Simple
Strategies
for
Business
Success

How to WIN at the game of business
and live life on YOUR terms!

SHARON PEARSON

THE COACHING
INSTITUTE

Published by Sharon Pearson
The Coaching Institute
335 Ferrars Street, South Melbourne, Victoria 3205 Australia

FIRST EDITION 2010

National Library of Australia Cataloguing-in-Publication entry
is available from the National Library of Australia Catalogue

Pearson, Sharon
Simple Strategies for Business Success : How to win at the game of
business and live life on your terms / Sharon Pearson

ISBN: 978-0-646-54292-8 (pbk.)

Printed in Australia by Fergies Print & Mail

Book design by Brett Geoghegan

To all business owners who went into it so
they could have life on their terms.

Contents

Foreword

It's with great excitement that I have been invited to write the forward for this great book.

Early in my career, someone gave me a piece of advice that has remained with me. Someone said 'there is two ways to live your life – one is through trial and error and the other is through following other peoples experiences'. Because whatever you want to do life, someone out there has already done it, or if not, done something very similar. They have invested a whole lot of time and money, made a lot of mistakes and eventually succeeded. So why would you waste your time trying to live your life through trial and error when you can instead go directly to the source and follow a proven success formula.

A challenge with this though is to make sure that you are following the advice of the right people, people that have produced proven and documented results. So now, as we come back to this book, it gives me great pleasure to introduce my good friend and mentor, Sharon Pearson.

Throughout publishing my series of best selling books, I've had the fantastic opportunity to work with over 214 of the country's most successful business owners and thought-leaders in a range of topic areas. Often I am asked who are the people that have impressed you most? Clearly, there's so many amazing people to choose from so it's a difficult thing to do. However when it comes to business, right at the top of the list would be Sharon Pearson.

What I love most about Sharon is she is the ultimate example of what's possible. With hard work, resilience and an obsessive passion for knowledge, she proves that it's possible for anyone to go from scratch to developing a multi-million dollar business.

For those that might be slightly skeptical, let me just say that Sharon Pearson is the real deal. I have visited her office on a number of occasions, met with her staff and we have had a number of intimate conversations about the inner workings of her business. So if you're looking to learn from someone who has walked in the shoes of experience and has the runs on the board, then you've found it.

In this book, your going to save yourself time and money and skip the fatal mistakes most business owners make. You will discover the power of a Millionaire Mindset and the secrets to sourcing the right mentor for ultimate success. Learn how to build systems that maximize your income and get you out of your business. And best of all – learn from Sharon who has been there and done that. Her knowledge in marketing will blow you away and you will find yourself referring back to his book over and over again.

On a final note, I want to encourage you to take the next step on your journey. It's one thing to read a book and be empowered with a whole lot of great information, but it's another thing to actually put it into action and follow through. Sharon has a number of additional materials and workshops (and I have attended many of them) so I encourage you to go to the website and discover how you can work with Sharon Pearson and her team of experts:

www.smallbusinessmastermindclub.com.au

Now enjoy the book and I hope to one day read about your success story.

DALE BEAUMONT
Creator of the *Secrets Exposed Series*
Author of 16 best selling books

Introduction

The only reason you'd read this book is if you're crazy enough to think you too can make it in business. You'd only read it if you want to fire your boss and have life on your terms. Otherwise, put it back on the shelf. Immediately.

Eight years ago I was insane enough to think I could make it in my own business. I was complete rubbish in the first year, the second year was pretty good and I made one million dollars in year three. My income has gone up since then, so it seems my insanity paid off.

I do have life on my terms, now.

I didn't. Not in year one. Certainly not in year two. Nope, not even in year three.

I only had the life I wanted when I learned what I've included in this book. It came down to changing my thinking, changing my marketing and building a business that could run without me, so I could actually have a life. Three separate ways of thinking that I had to learn the hard way. Maybe you won't make the mistakes I made. Maybe you'll pause for a moment from working your duff off, and learn how to skip the mistakes, so instead of eight years, you can do it in three years.

One client took what's in this book and did their first million in 7 months. Amazing what's possible when you get the right information at the right time.

This is the right time for you if you:

- Are tired of struggling in your business
- Work hard for mediocre results
- Know it should be easier
- Want to get out of that job and into living life on your terms
- Are ready to accelerate your business profits in the next 30 to 90 days.

I've made it a highly 'consumable' book – short chapters so you can grab a section here or there and apply it immediately. I've also included templates and checklists to accompany many of the chapters so you can take action whilst it's fresh in your mind.

And it's all designed to get you your life, on your terms, exactly as you want it to be.

Business can be simple. My experience – I've worked with over 2,000 people who have started out in business and wanted better results, faster – tells me that far too many business owners are making things tough for themselves - and unnecessarily so.

Why are you in business? What's the overriding aim of your business? No, I don't mean things like capturing a certain percentage of the market, or reaching a turnover figure of such and such. There's only one answer here. Every business exists for one reason only: to add value. That's it, straight and simple.

If you don't add value, you don't make a profit. If you don't make a profit, you don't stay in business. Your first and foremost thought every day and the thing that must drive all decisions in your business is how to provide more value.

If you don't achieve this goal, then you aren't in business – you have a hobby.

To provide more value you need three things: the right mindset, the right marketing machine and the right business systems. This book is divided into three parts so you can access those three critical elements easily.

- Developing Your Millionaire Mindset.
- Your Marketing System for Massive Success.
- How to Build the Systems To Get You OUT of Your Business.

I'm going to show you how to find out what your clients and prospective clients want more than anything. Then I'm going to show you how to get in front of them, 24/7. Then I'm going to walk you through how to make massive profits, day in, day out.

A good month for me is making over $750,000. A bad month is making $250,000. Yes, I'm talking profit. And I work part time. My business is running for me as I write this book.

It's called **'value-based marketing'** and it forms the basis of everything we do in our business.

Our product development is based only on what our clients and prospects want more than anything. We don't build a better mouse trap and hope they'll come. We discover what they want, and that's what we build. It's strategic, there's no guesswork and it works.

Once you stop building mouse traps and instead build a 'value-based' business, you'll find all the business you can handle will come your way.

Yes, there's more to business than that; but the fact remains that the basic concept of business is a simple one. Perhaps it is deceptively simple; perhaps it is so simple that most business owners miss the point completely. And perhaps this is one of the reasons they find running a business such a complex, all-consuming thing.

But it needn't be that way.

I know, because I have discovered that for myself. I learnt the hard way. But before I get to that, let me tell you another startling thing I have discovered about business and those who practice it. I have found that there are really only two types of people who go into business for themselves: those who already know (or manage to discover) the secrets of having a business that works for them instead of the other way round, and everyone else. And I'm sure I don't need to tell you into which camp the vast majority of them fall.

It also explains why the vast majority of business owners end up working their guts out chasing their tails and getting nowhere. After all, what's the point of taking all the risks by giving up a full-time job only to become the lowest paid, hardest working person on the team? You'd be surprised at how many business owners only pay themselves what's left over after paying their team, the bills and their suppliers. They end up working hard because their business doesn't.

The statistics are frightening. Most small businesses fail within five years of starting up – what's worse, even if they survive, a staggering number of business owners are destined to barely scrape a living together. For them, what started out as a bright dream of a life of freedom and abundance turns into a nightmare of struggle and frustration.

Perhaps this sounds familiar to someone you know well.

But it doesn't have to be that way for you. You can be in that fortunate first group of people living life on your own terms and having a successful business that provides you with the money and the freedom to make your dreams come true.

Still a little sceptical? That's fine. You see, you have already taken the first step towards living life on your terms by buying this book. And by beginning to read it, you have taken the second step.

So why would I share what I know about building a successful business? I share it because I want you to skip the fatal mistakes that too many business owners make and I want you to become a part of our community of successful business owners – people who are just like you – who wanted to have life on their terms and didn't know how. They used what's in this book and it changed how they did business forever. You can read about their success stories here:

www.smallbusinessmastermindclub.com.au/case-studies

I'm the founder of The Coaching Institute. That's a business that went from just an idea to being the leading provider of training for coaches in Australia in less than three years. It's now a multi-million dollar business. I grew it from $12,000 in the first year to $10 million in turnover in under five years. The Coaching Institute won the Telstra Micro Business Award, and I'm a Telstra Business Women's Award finalist.

Before that, I set up a direct marketing business that generated sales of over $1 million in the first year and had over 50 employees.

I tell you this to show you that I know what I'm talking about when it comes to building a real business. Today, I really am living my dream and enjoying great success. But it wasn't always like this. In fact, for quite a while I struggled like many people do in business. I knew I needn't continue to struggle and I was driven to discover the 'secret' to success in business. I knew it had to exist because some business owners seemed to be sailing through life so easily. And if they could, then why couldn't I?

So I set out to achieve my goals of a life of freedom and independence, armed with a lot of enthusiasm and bright ideas, but (unfortunately) not a lot of real-world business savvy.

The result, to start, with was miserable failure and bitter disappointment. But, fortunately, I'm not the kind of person who gives up easily. So I set out to uncover exactly how to start and build a business from experts who had a proven track record in the real world of business.

I attended dozens of seminars and joined several high-end coaching programs. I spent tens of thousands of dollars and months of my life on the best business education available. But you know something? Even that wasn't enough, because a lot of what I needed to know wasn't being taught by anyone.

So I realised there was no other option; I had to find out for myself through trial and error.

Part of the problem, I realised, was that we were in a so-called 'new economy'. The Internet had opened up vast new opportunities to build a business faster and more easily than ever before. And because it was so new, it took a while to discover the techniques and tactics that really worked consistently. There were many traps for the beginner and blind alleys that lead nowhere (believe me, I probably made every mistake there was to make). It took time and effort, but once I figured things out, my business really took off and I've never looked back.

Now, I can't possibly assist every business owner who comes to me wanting me to share how to build a value-based business, so I have condensed much of the information I learned into this easy-to-read book that you can dip in and out of on an on-going basis to help guide the way as you navigate your way through business. Follow the simple suggestions it outlines, and you too will be able to live life on your own terms.

So congratulations on taking these first steps towards a better life. You won't regret it; that I guarantee.

PART I:

Developing your millionaire mindset

1

The ultimate determinant of your success

We can have more than we've got because we can become more than we are.

JIM ROHN

When you really think about it, one of the main reasons anyone goes into business is to achieve a level of lifestyle for themselves and their families. You want to provide a living, but more than that you want to make your dreams become a reality.

You want to have a life on your terms.

The other reason most of us go into business for ourselves is because we think we can do it. There needs to be a sustained note of insanity that drives us to launch into the complete unknown, inexperienced, under resourced and with nothing but the hope that we can crank things up before the cash dries up.

Let's face it, the vast majority of people simply don't have the discipline to go it alone. Then there is the whole question of being a jack-of-all-trades. Particularly in the early stages the hopeful and clueless business owner finds themselves doing absolutely everything themselves.

Madness.

Go get a job. Make it easier for yourself. Give up. This is hard. This is a path that is covered with the gutted dreams of failed business owners that came before you and didn't make it. What are you thinking?

Still here?

Congratulations. Then let's get you mentally prepared.

Business can be fun. It can be exhilarating. It can be exciting, energising and every other superlative you can think of. If you know what you're doing.

There are rules to business, there are rules to how you think and there are rules to how you make decisions.

Setting out on the path to success in business is the first step to setting out to success in life. It will give you the momentum, the means and the stamina to achieve your life goals. And it will help you do so far quicker than if you were to remain locked into a job.

The important thing is to see this as part of your overall life journey. Your business is nothing more than a means to an end. It's the vehicle that makes your dreams and goals come true. So with this in mind, I want you to think about this: have you achieved everything you want out of life right now?

Whatever decision you took sometime in the past has come to be, or influenced what is, today. If you took different decisions in the past, your present would be very different from the one you have right now. Do you like where you're at? Is business what you want it to be? Are you doing what you want to, when you want to, and how you want to?

To live life on your terms – to be able to live the life of your dreams – you need to have an understanding of what you want from life. This begins, of course, with knowing where you are on that journey to start with. It also presupposes that you know what you hold to be true and it's worth striving for. It also demands that you are in touch with your emotions and know how to deal with, and overcome, fear.

Perhaps the most powerful and empowering characteristic of humans is that we have the power of choice. We really are in a wonderful position to be able to CHOOSE what we want and don't want out of life. Each and every day we make choices. This is powerful, because it means that if you are not happy with where you are at in life right now, you only have to choose to do things differently from this point on. This means you have the gift of making new beginnings whenever you want to. You get to start all over again if you are not entirely satisfied with the way things are for you right now. You get to change things you aren't happy with.

This is the first part of the millionaire mindset. It's your choices and non choices that have got you where you are.

It's your choices and non choices that will get you where you're going. And whether you like the outcomes, or not, it's down to you and your choices.

If you choose NOT to choose, that in itself is still a choice – so you really can't escape it. You have to make choices whether you like it or not.

The thing is, then, how well are you choosing? What are you choosing? The ultimate determinant of your success is what your choose and what you don't choose.

It would be so much easier if I was to say: 'It's not your fault.' In fact, most marketers worth their salt know to NEVER blame the prospect for what's going wrong with them. It's Marketing 101: It's not the prospect's fault.

But this isn't about blame, or fault. It's about choice. It's about realising that unless we take responsibility for our choices, we can't influence our results.

Making smart choices

For your business to work, and for you to develop a millionaire mindset, you need to make smart choices that are going to move you forward. Sometimes they're hard choices, but they're the right choices because they're going to get you the end game – life on your terms.

If everything in life came down to being a series of choices, would now be a good time to make choices that empower you? That lead you to success? That would propel you closer to where you want your life to be? If you gave any other answer than: right now, go take a nap.

Take the time right now to write down some new choices that will empower you, lead to new results, allow you to get rid of some things you have been tolerating, give you the freedom to act, to learn, to grow, to discover what you're really made of.

Write each new choice this way: I now choose …

So for instance, your list of choices may look something like this:

- I now choose to believe in myself
- I now choose to do the things that will move this business forward
- I now choose to take myself lightly
- I now choose to get educated on business success
- I now choose to focus on what needs fixing
- I now choose to give up complaining and blaming
- I now choose to get my finances in order and face some truths
- I now choose to build a business that gives me life on my terms
- I now choose to book that holiday for six month's time, because by then my business will be in the sweet spot!

What are the positive consequences of these choices? What will your life look like in three years from now? Five years? Ten years if you keep making choices like this?

The secret here lies in the way you think about things. Every self-made millionaire I have got to know sees themselves, not fate or luck, as the reason for where they're at. They are seeking constantly to make better decisions.

They are always searching for new ways of looking at things so they can make even better choices.

It's no coincidence that the people who are already successful are the same people who join the high-end coaching groups, even though they know nearly everything that is being taught in the room. They know that it's the tiny distinctions that will make a big difference – small hinges swing big doors.

To be a millionaire you need to adopt the same attitude about you and your business. Take responsibility for your choices, and constantly learn how to improve the choices you make.

The three levels of Your Success

The Your Success philosophy holds that there are three levels at which we can be living our lives. Whichever level we decide to live determines the quality of our life. Whichever level we live our life at comes down to a choice.

Look at each of these levels and determine which level you are choosing to live your life at. You may be living at different levels depending upon the area of your life you think about. For example, you may be living at Level I in health and Level III in business.

If your finances are pretty bad, then you'll probably relate to Level III thinking around them.

Self made millionaires are living in Level I when it comes to their wealth, their business and their success.

Level III thinking

Level III living is where we are invested in the stories of 'why we can't'; and these stories prevent us from experiencing the results we desire. A story is anything we tell ourselves to justify not creating transformation. For example, someone may say, "I can't be a successful salesperson because my parents never taught me how to communicate." Or, "I don't succeed in relationships because my work is too important." Or, "My bad back stops me succeeding in business." Or, "If you'd been abused like I was, you wouldn't be happy either." Or, "I'm too old to learn anything new, and that's why I don't succeed."

Anything that you tell yourself is the reason for not being able to act or to take responsibility is your story. It is what you drag around with you as your escape clause. I don't say this to be harsh, because I have done this myself, and on occasions I still do. Learning this stuff isn't a one-time deal. You don't learn it and then everything is perfect in your life and business. We each need to hold ourselves accountable to being aware of when we buy into these stories. The story I dragged around for years was, "I can't be successful because I have too many issues from my past to deal with."

The amount of time you spend investing in your stories is the amount of time you aren't investing in getting your life on your terms. The more time you spend at this level is less time you have to build your ideal life, because your thoughts are filled with the language of excuses and of feelings of lack and of self-doubt.

People who live mostly at this level tend to wonder why they are stuck and can't get on with their lives. They hope things will get better. They don't believe in much because life has given them so little to believe in.

Level III living means taking responsibility when it is convenient and surrendering responsibility when the going gets tough.

Level III living includes why we can't be our ideal weight or have an extraordinary relationship. It is about what we tell ourselves people have done to us and it's about blame. What we tell ourselves prevents us from getting ahead – you know: I'm not old enough; I'm too old; not enough training; not enough education; not good enough parents; no money. In fact, that last story – not enough money – is one of the more common stories I hear.

Level II thinking

If you are living at Level II, you are aware that there are some areas in your life that need changing but you're not sure how to go about creating the change. You would experience confusion and self-doubt. Level II people create change for themselves if they are presented with a means of how to turn things around but don't always actively go find the solutions. Level II people often think life could be better, but rather than just hoping it improves, like Level III people, they seek out the answers – as long as they don't have to change too much themselves.

Level II people might be into alternative remedies and alternative solutions, because the mainstream answers have proven disappointing. They might believe in astrology and psychics. These are 'solutions' outside of themselves so they are not responsible.

While Level II people have stories they tell themselves about why their life isn't exactly as they want it, they still experience levels of happiness and success. Their stories haven't become all they have, so their level of scepticism and their disappointment in the world isn't as ingrained as it might be for someone at Level III.

Those at Level II might take responsibility for some areas of their lives, especially the areas they are good at, or in which they feel most comfortable. When they take responsibility, they like how it feels and want to do it more. But when they don't find something easy, or they struggle to 'get it', or it's a stretch, they revert back to Level III thinking, where it's easier to blame circumstance.

Level I thinking

Level I people know that it is entirely up to them what happens in their lives. They hold themselves 100% responsible for the results they get, regardless of what the results might be – because they know that anything less is giving away their opportunity to affect change.

Someone operating at Level I would never indulge in blame or justification, because they know that doing so simply stops them learning and growing from a situation. They know that through growing and learning they become even more successful. They aren't interested in whom to blame, but rather how to turn the situation around.

Level I people feel gratitude for what they have in their lives, including their opportunities to learn and grow. They see problems as gifts for them to take their lives to the next level.

Someone at Level I doesn't bemoan the past, but has forgiven whoever they perceive harmed them knowing that the act of forgiveness is a gift for themselves.

Level I living is an extraordinary level of self-responsibility. It isn't about blame, but choice.

Level I living is about taking yourself lightly, and looking for the good in every situation.

Level I living embraces the five keys we are about to look at all of the time, not just when it is convenient.

2

The keys to success

The person who gets the farthest is generally the one who is willing to do and dare. The sure-thing boat never gets far from shore.

DALE CARNEGIE

Key Number One: You must take control of how you interpret your world

Millionaires already know that what determines the quality of your life is not what happens: your level of luck or hard times, your family, your income, your job or your friends. What determines the quality of your life is the meaning you give to the events that happen and the choices you make as a result of those meanings.

Throughout the world there are people who we know (or know of) who have overcome extraordinary hardships, loss or challenges and gone on to live remarkable lives. Despite their own suffering, they have found a way to live lives of fulfilment and have made a difference to our world. Throughout history, people have made incredible sacrifices to achieve extraordinary success.

For years, people held the belief that it was impossible for a human being to run the mile in less than four minutes. Then Roger Bannister did exactly that in 1954. He achieved the 'impossible' through mental and physical practice.

What is remarkable about this story goes far beyond what Bannister achieved. Within one year of his feat, 37 other runners broke the four-minute mile. A year after that, another 300 runners did the same thing.

Had four minutes become a longer time? No. Had a mile shrunk to accommodate the runners? No. All that had changed was what people believed was possible.

What this tells us is that it isn't the event that has meaning. We can never see an event exactly for what it is. Our interpretation of an event is all we have.

Even if we try really hard to only interpret an event for what it is, we will still distort the event in our minds to conform with what we believe to be true. This means that "the map is not the territory". No matter how hard we endeavour to recreate an event or a situation, we will only be able to represent it based on our map of the world.

This one key has the power to totally transform your life. It's not the events in your life that shape you, it's the meaning you give these events.

W Mitchell was 28 years old when it happened. He was travelling along a highway on his new motorbike when something caught his eyes. And when he looked back in the direction in which he was travelling, the laundry truck in front of him suddenly came to a stop.

The bike went down, crushing his elbow and pelvis. The gas cap popped off; fuels was ignited by the heat of the engine and the next thing he remembers is that he's in hospital, with three-quarter of his body covered by terrible third degree burns.

When he arrived, doctors were not even sure if he would survive. He was judged to have little chance of recovery and his face had been burned beyond recognition.

He survived only after numerous operations – including 16 skin grafts, and 13 transfusions.

Apart from his physical appearance, all his fingers and thumbs had been burnt off in the accident and he was left with two stumps where his hands used to be.

During this time be communicated to himself that the accident had happened for a purpose. And within six months of the accident, he was back on his feet again and had co-founded a wood-stove company which went on to become Vermont's second largest employer.

His personal wealth climbed to three million dollars. He purchased a home and a personal airplane. He also made a name for himself in politics, became the town's Mayor for two terms and ran for Congress – despite the fact that his face was grotesquely scarred.

His slogan: "Send me to Congress, and I won't be just another pretty face."

Despite having stumps instead of hands, he got his pilot's licence.

Then, in a routine flight, ice formed on the wings. The plane crashed. Everyone got out except him. 12 vertebrae were completely crushed and his spinal cord was beyond repair. He would never use his legs again.

This is what he said: "Before my accidents, there were ten thousand things I could do. I could spend the rest of my life dwelling on the one thousand that I had lost, but I instead choose to focus on the nine thousand I still have left."

Despite having no hands and not being able to walk, he continues to live a full life. He's the director of the board to a number of companies, and is a successful businessman. He is also a co-founding chairman of a $65 million company.

He enjoys sky diving and white water rafting.

Key Number Two: You must believe it's possible

Scientists used to believe that we responded to information that flowed into our brains from the world around us. Today they're learning instead that we actually respond to what our brain, on the basis of previous experience, expects to happen next.

Neuropsychologists who study expectancy theory say we spend our whole lives becoming conditioned – our brain expects something to happen a certain way, so that's what we look for, and that's what we get.

Two years after an 'operation' where nothing but an incision was made in a patient's knee whilst they were anesthetised, the patient reported the same amount of relief from pain and swelling as those who received the actual treatment.

The brain expected the knee to be improved, so it was.

I believe what you expect to happen will override any efforts you're making. If you don't expect success, all the hours you're doing are going to count for little.

Tony Robbins, world renowned peak performance expert, says, "Any time you sincerely want to make a change, you must raise your standards. Change what you demand of yourself."

Our beliefs are like unquestioned commands to ourselves about what is possible. They shape our actions, our thoughts, our responses and our results. Change your beliefs about what you can achieve and you will change what you do. Change what you do, and you'll get a different result.

And it just might be the result you were looking for.

It's not our events that shape us, but our beliefs about what these events mean. And we determine that for ourselves. The fastest way to change our beliefs and expectations of what is possible is to be around and learn from people who have already experienced the success you want.

I made a huge effort to immerse myself in the world of Tony Robbins, Jack Canfield and others who had already achieved massive success in similar arenas to me. It's little wonder that their 'magic' rubbed off on me. Each day when I exercised I loaded up my MP3, did my "Hour of Power" and drank in from the their deep wells of knowledge.

Constant repetition, week after week, of how to think, what to believe and what to expect, eventually overruled thirty something years of lack, fear and disbelief.

I 'reconditioned' myself to expect success.

I was a millionaire two years after that.

Key Number Three: Take 100% responsibility for the results you get

There is only one person responsible for the quality of life you live.

If you truly want to be successful then you simply must take 100% responsibility for everything you experience in your life. This includes the stuff you love and the stuff you can't stand. It include the quality of your relationships, your feelings, the state of your health and the state of your finances.

This isn't easy.

Most of us are conditioned to blame something outside of ourselves for the bits of our lives that aren't working. We blame our parents, our lack of education, bad luck, bad boss, bad economy, our lack of money – anyone or anything that isn't us.

Jack Canfield, co author of the *Chicken Soup* series of best sellers, shares how he had the privilege of working for W. Clement Stone – a self-made millionaire worth $600 million at the time (1969) – publisher of Success magazine and author of The Success System That Never Fails.

One week into his job Mr. Stone asked Jack if he took 100% responsibility for his life.

Jack answered: I think so.

Mr. Stone told him it was either a yes or no answer. There were no 'maybes'. He asked him if he had ever blamed anyone for any circumstance in his life or ever complained about anything.

Jack Canfield confessed that, yes, he had.

To which Mr. Stone replied: That means you don't take 100% responsibility for your life. Taking 100% responsibility means you acknowledge that you create everything that happens to you. It means that you understand that you are cause of everything that happens.

If you want to be successful, you have to give up blaming, complaining and examining history for what went wrong. If you realise that you created your results, then you can realise you can change them.

To do this, you have to give up your excuses, your victim stories and all the reasons you've been using to convince yourself that it's not your fault.

You might not be able to change the outcome, but you can definitely change your response to it, and what you do next.

Key Number Four: You must get rid of the secondary gain

Have you ever done something that is harmful to yourself, recognised that it's harmful, and kept doing it? It could be a recurring negative thought about yourself, such as, 'I'm not good enough'. It could be behaviour like not returning the phone calls or keeping the finances up to date. It could manifest itself as self-sabotage. Perhaps you want to save some money

– and then, the moment you get ahead, you blow your entire earnings on something you hardly need.

You know you're crazy blowing the savings. In fact, you've done it before and you are aware of the price you will have to pay, but you do it anyway.

Why?

Because of secondary gain. On some level, you get a 'reward' for doing that crazy thing. You get a reward for eating the extra piece of cake, even though you're trying to lose weight for that special occasion. You get a reward for missing that deadline at work. You get a reward for saying you'll do one thing and then doing something else instead.

The 'reward' or 'payoff' is that you get to feel what you really want to feel, or you get to avoid a feeling you don't want.

For example, you don't call the client. Even though you know they are going to be unhappy with you not calling them, you make sure you're doing something else at that time, and tell yourself: It's not that important.

You get to feel in control of your environment, because you made the choice to not make the call. And equally importantly, you get to avoid the feeling of self-doubt you would have had if you'd called and they'd given you a hard time.

It makes sense to make the call, because it's only going to get worse, but you put it off. The 'benefit' of avoiding the call is perceived as greater than the 'benefit' of dealing with it head on.

This secondary gain has the ability to keep us doing, saying and thinking what we know is completely wrong for us. It keeps us eating the extra cake. It keeps us skipping that morning walk. It keeps us avoiding doing what needs to be done to fix our business. And we do this crazy stuff because on some level it works for us to do so.

No exceptions. If you skip the responsibility, it worked for you to do so. Ask yourself, "Why did you do it?" If the answer is: "I don't know... it's probably because of secondary gain.

On some level, you perceive a benefit from this seemingly unwanted behaviour.

Don't bother telling yourself right now that you are the exception to the payoff rule. There are no exceptions to this rule.

I coached a client once who insisted he wanted to become a better time manager. He would articulate how his poor time skills were costing him so much. He expressed total commitment to changing his behaviour; yet, within a day, he was back to his old patterns.

Why? Because on some level staying with the old choice was working for him. By being a poor timekeeper, he didn't have to do what was needed to improve his business, because he was too busy trying to manage his time.

The payoff for his poor time management skills was his not having to be real about where is business was at. And as long as he didn't have to face it, he didn't have to take responsibility for it. Responsibility was scary for him. The drama of bad time management was not scary, and provided a perfect distraction for him from the real issues.

You could decide to study to get better at running your business, or just because it's something you're interested in. Yet the enrolment time comes around, and you do nothing. You tell yourself that you'll do it next semester, or that no one will appreciate your efforts, or that no one your age gets great results, or it's been years since you studied, so you'll be the worst in the class.

You know the study is important. It makes perfect sense to get into that class. But you didn't join. Why? Because then there would be no excuses for not succeeding. There would be nothing and no one to blame. It would be on you, and that's scary. Much less scary to say you're too busy and you'll do it next year.

The key to this is appreciating that we do more to avoid pain than we do to feel pleasure. This is true for all of us, and the level by which we live our lives determines our willingness to tolerate pain.

Level III players avoid pain, or risk, at all costs. Level II players will take some risks, if they can manage them. Level I players take risks, because they know that if they don't succeed, at least they had a go.

We do more to avoid pain than we do to feel pleasure.

Psychologists have understood this key for years. We want to avoid the feelings of failure, of self-doubt, of lack of confidence. We don't want to fail, look silly, risk being rejected, or any of the other fears we hold in our heads. The benefit of playing it safe is we get to avoid all of this perceived pain.

If you want something in your business to turn around and find yourself falling short at the last moment (or justifying why you're not doing it or avoiding it), then you are in the grasp of secondary gain. You perceive the pain of changing greater than the pain of things staying the same and not improving.

Most secondary gain is a fear of going outside our comfort zones. We fear the unknown. We fear not seeing how we can control every step that lies ahead of us. We want to have certainty about how things will play out before we act.

Because things would change if we changed our behaviour, we get scared and don't change. We could stop being late all the time, but then we wouldn't be able to blame lateness for stuff that's overlooked. If we didn't have that to blame, we'd have to take responsibility for the stuff we'd been overlooking. Things would have to improve, and with the improvements, there would be more responsibility. Easier instead to stay being late.

We thing we want things to stay the same so we can stay comfortable. Or so we think.

Imagine a life in which you knew in advance how everything that was going to happen to you, played out. Imagine that you knew exactly what you had to do. Imagine that you could see every move every time.

You would hate it, because even though we think we want certainty about how things will unfold, what we want even more is to be challenged so we can find out what we are capable of.

You are not designed to play it safe. You are designed as a learning machine. You have the capability to learn and apply intricate moves that are beyond even the most advanced computers on the planet. You have more neural pathways in your brain than there are grains of sand on every beach on the planet. You were built to test yourself because, when you do, you discover what you are capable of – and it's only when you learn that, you feel happy and fulfilled.

The only way to feel happy is to feel the fear and to act regardless of it.

You can't get happy playing it safe. You certainly can't become a millionaire. It is impossible to feel a sense of accomplishment sitting still and convincing yourself that the risk isn't worth it. Every time you talk yourself out of attempting a new thing, you move a step further away from the person you truly are.

Secondary gain is you telling yourself that you're better off not stepping up.

We all do it; but remember: it's what we do consistently that makes the difference. If you consistently listen to the 'play-it-safe' voice, you are living at Level III. If you listen to the 'play-it-safe' voice most of the time, you are living at Level II. If you hear the voice but do it anyway, you are playing at Level I.

You will experience the results you want in your business and a personal sense of accomplishment because you know you have courage. You back yourself.

Playing it safe teaches us apathy and mediocrity. No one can learn that they have courage by playing it safe. The only way to find out if you have courage is to act when you feel fear.

Now back to secondary gain. When the opportunities presented to you throughout life get sifted through the filter system in your mind as being scary, painful and risky, it's easy to become frozen in inaction. Then you start to normalise your backing away from the opportunity by telling yourself something like, 'I didn't want it anyway', or 'I'm better off sticking to what I know'.

There's the payoff. The benefit is you get to hide from the truth – the truth about what you are capable of – and you avoid the pain of the fear of failing or of succeeding, or whatever it is for you.

This starts to breed the lack of self-confidence that so many people say they experience in their businesses every day. This, then, reinforces non-action – because how can people be expected to act when they have low self-esteem?

"Yep, I'd love to throw myself into the sales process and make those calls but I really have low self-confidence; what if no one wants to talk with me?"

"Sure, I'd ask for that account if I wasn't so shy; but you know how it is."

These are examples of perfect excuses to not play the game of life – except the only person it hurts is you.

One of the things I constantly say to my clients is that the only question I care about when mentoring is 'what works?'.

If telling ourselves we have low self-esteem was a strategy that worked, then I'd say go for it; but I am yet to meet a client who has a million dollar business and plays at Level III with their excuses.

If telling yourself, 'I can't' gets you what you want in life, then you keep doing it. I'm going to guess, though, it doesn't and suggest an alternative strategy.

Everyone has self-doubts and fear. Everyone wonders if they will have what it takes. No exceptions. The difference between Level III and Level I players is that Level III players let it stop them and Level I players don't.

Why passively accept the excuses you've told yourself if all they do is keep you from having the wealth you want and deserve?

I worked with a client who said he really wanted to learn how to communicate better with the people in his company. He didn't change his behaviour towards anyone until he gave up his secondary gain of needing to be the centre of attention whenever there was a drama or confrontation.

Another client of mine said she wanted to build her business. That didn't happen until she came to identify and release her payoff. As long as she wasn't succeeding in business, she kept saying that 'it's never going to happen for me'. By saying this my client got to stay safe. Her payoff was she didn't have to risk putting herself on the line.

So how can you learn to let go of secondary gain?

The first step to letting go of the payoffs is to get real about what they are. Any area of your life where you have told yourself you want it to be different but haven't changed is worth looking at.

Identify the area you want to improve. Then answer these questions:

- What do you tell yourself about why it isn't how you want it?

- What has been the payoff for you not playing at Level I until now?

- What has the secondary gain prevented you from being, doing, having or experiencing

- What don't you have in your life because you have had the secondary gain?

- What do you have that you don't want in your life because of it?

- What action are you going to take now that you have identified the secondary gain?

- What is going to be different from now on?

The second step to move through the secondary gain is to hold yourself accountable when you become aware of it returning. Playing Level I living is about knowing that the buck stops with you.

How will you make sure you continue to play at Level I? For example, will you tell someone you trust to hold you accountable if you ever fall back into one of your old patterns of behaviour? Will you write down your goals and make sure you follow through?

Key Number Five: You must be willing to explore – and embrace – the unfamiliar

All the talk in the world about what we can do to transform our financial results is just talk, unless we are willing to explore how to do things differently for ourselves. Knowledge is only knowledge if we apply it; otherwise, it's just information gathering.

I know someone who would rather feel totally in control of her life than anything else. It is more important for her to know what is going to happen every minute of the day than to learn something new or to explore the unfamiliar. This means she has a safe job that delivers few surprises. She also has very few friends; people scare her because they are unpredictable. It also means she can't handle feedback, so getting ahead in her organisation is difficult. She also prefers to be right rather than learn a new and better way to do something.

Compare this to someone who embraces the unknown and is willing to learn. Imagine the quality of life of someone who likes to discover the unknown and make it known, and who doesn't have to be right all the time. They are happy to learn new and better ways to do things. They aren't threatened by change or the unfamiliar, but are curious to know more about it and integrate it into their ever-expanding understanding of themselves and their world.

One client adopted this attitude during their five day Mastermind training – she did $50,000 in business in the two weeks straight after the event.

Life is uncertain. There is no escaping this, and the more effort we put into getting rid of the uncertainty, the more energy we're wasting. Instead of trying to control the inevitable, what about focusing on what you can control and influence? Focus, instead, on what you enjoy, what you can do, what your strengths are, and what you want to achieve.

The fact is, in life, there are few guarantees. You can't control your world. You have no control over the future. This sounds negative, but in reality it's freeing. Think about it. If you accept this is true, doesn't it free you to focus on what you can control?

It is only in the unknown that one can learn. Think about this for a moment. If you already know something, isn't it in the realm of the known? If you don't know something, isn't it in the realm of the unknown?

So many people fear the unknown. They will do anything to avoid it, including insisting they know best, that what they've been doing gets them by, that they don't need anything else, or they delete any evidence that things are not fine.

Think about a situation in your own business that left you feeling anxious. Perhaps it was the need to learn a new skill or capability. Perhaps you needed to talk to someone you didn't know and you weren't sure how to do it. Perhaps you had to stretch yourself beyond what you were certain you could do.

How did you feel? What did you do? Did you keep going or back off? And, after that, did you avoid similar situations or seek them out?

Most people will say they avoid situations that involve them venturing outside their comfort zone. Yet, the only way to create the change we want in our life is to go to what I call the 'uncomfort zone'.

The income you earn is directly proportional to the amount of uncertainty you can handle. The more uncertainty you enjoy, the more new things you'll be open to experiencing, so the more results you'll have.

What's so great about a comfort zone? What is so appealing about playing it safe, living within the square, thinking the same, acting the same, and doing what you did yesterday (and the day before that)?

Our company used to attend a personal development exhibition in two cities each year. We offered people who are interested the opportunity to win a coach or become a coach. They have the chance to win $1000 of coaching where they can learn about themselves and who they are. Even if they don't win, they can still have a free coaching session, compliments of our school. The session is valued at $200 and gives anyone the opportunity to discover more about themselves and what it is they want to focus on for the year ahead.

What intrigues me is that as the doors to the exhibition open and the crowd rushes in —hundreds of people — they all make the dash to the stand they have come to see: the fortune tellers.

What they want is certainty; certainty about how their lives will work out; certainty they will experience love; certainty they will succeed. Certainty. Certainty. Certainty.

Instead of realising that all possibilities exist in their lives, they rather choose to invest in one possibility: a possibility predicted by someone else. And some of these people act on these predictions. What I am saying is that looking for certainty in our future is surrendering our greatest gift — the ability to enjoy the ride regardless of where it takes us.

How do we do this? We give up the need to be right. We surrender the desire to win an argument, to prove a point, to correct someone else, or remind ourselves of our expertise. If you have a big case of 'certainitis', then this will be a stretch for you, as it was for me. It's worth sticking at, though, because you'll start to relax and go with the flow. You'll notice people's differences with appreciation, instead of desiring to change them to conform to your way of thinking.

Get used to saying 'maybe'. Instead of having to know the answer, get in the habit of being curious about what all the possibilities could be. If someone says to you, 'this won't work', suppress the need to say how it will, or why you think it won't. Instead say, even if it's just to yourself, 'maybe …', or 'I wonder …', or 'let's see …'. For example, instead of saying 'I hope this works out', say 'I wonder how it works out'. Instead of saying 'I hope I get the account, say 'I wonder if I'll get the account. Instead of saying 'I wish this was better', say 'I wonder how this can be improved'. Instead of saying 'I wish this was easier', say 'I'm curious about how to do it easier'.

Do you notice the difference in how you feel when you say these sentences?

Why have your dreams dashed by using the word 'hope', when you can simply satisfy your curiosity by 'wondering' about something? It's much less a drama, and it eliminates the stories we tell ourselves.

Get curious about what you don't know. The one secret to growth, success and living life on your terms is to be curious about what is on the other side of your comfort zone. Be prepared to commit to stepping outside the walls of your comfort zone at least once a day. You will be amazed at how differently you start to view your world.

Acknowledge yourself. Even if you take one tiny step, take the time to acknowledge yourself for doing it. So few people praise themselves; this is why they don't like themselves. Would you like or be attracted to someone you didn't admire in some way? You're no different. You are worthy of your acknowledgement. Acknowledge yourself each day for what you have attempted and what you have accomplished. But perhaps more importantly, acknowledge yourself for who you are.

What do you recognise that you need to give up? Is it about being right? List what you need to surrender to move closer to Level I living.

Think of at least five things you might have said, 'I hope' to. For example, 'I hope I get the client, or 'I hope they choose me'.

Change them to 'I wonder' statements and notice the difference.

Think of five things you would like to explore that are, at the moment, outside of your comfort zone? What would change in your life if you did explore them? How would your life be improved?

Each day, commit to one action that takes you outside your comfort zone. If you're not sure what that might be, borrow some ideas from this list.

I could …

- Get on line
- Learn about value-based marketing

- Join a Mastermind Club
- Join a class on business
- Invite some potential clients over to a wine and cheese night
- Listen to some self-improvement CDs
- De-clutter the office
- Dress to impress
- Book and go on a holiday
- Start a home-based business
- Find a mentor who already has the results I want and learn from them
- Learn how to speak in public
- Read
- Learn something new
- Join a short course
- Write an article about something
- Donate some time to a worthy cause
- Design a new system
- Commit to one kind act each day
- Remind a child how phenomenal they are.

The more you depend on forces outside of yourself, the more they dominate you.

This is the challenge: for the next ten days, play your game of life as if each of the five keys were 100% correct. Remember, it isn't what you do – it's what you do *consistently* that determines whether you will get to truly live life on your terms.

Everything is an opportunity to learn – there is no failure, only feedback.

If you find yourself slipping in one area, remember: it is but a choice to get back on track. One slip into old habits is not who you are; it is simply an opportunity to step up once more. You will feel great about yourself when you do this.

How else will you play the game of life at level I?

3

Tapping into your super powers

Most people never run far enough on their first wind to find out they've got a second. Give your dreams all you've got and you'll be amazed at the energy that comes out of you.

WILLIAM JAMES

I am absolutely convinced that any success I have experienced, both in business and life, is due largely to how I think. I also know with certainty that the opposite is also true: the lack of success I have experienced at times has also been due to what was going on in my mind at the time.

I don't blame luck, chance, wrong timing, poor circumstances, the economy or my parents for what happens in my business. It's not the season, the political landscape or that Saturn is in Jupiter.

I choose to believe that you are 'at cause' for what happens – you determine your response to everything. No one is making you feel, think, decide or do anything – only you dictate you.

You shape your reality. Your thinking, your focus, your predominant thoughts and your emotions shape how you will experience your world every day.

Understand that wealth exists. Right now there is billions of dollars on this planet. The question isn't 'what's available?' it's 'what do you perceive as being available to you?' Right now.

When I thought that making money was hard, it was hard. When I learned how to attract money, and keep it, and I took action, it was easy. Which reality is accurate?

There is a mindset that wealthy people have. Think of any wealthy person and you'll see what I mean. Take Richard Branson, for example. What is your immediate impression of him that springs to mind? His carefree attitude? His smile? The 'aura of success' that he has? Whatever impression you get, it's probably connected somehow to success, isn't it? It probably relates to his mindset. Why do you think he is so successful with everything he does? Money? Not so. You see, he started with nothing. No money. Zilch. So it can't be money that got him to where he is today. It was (and still is) his mindset.

Let me give you another example.

I've been studying Tony Robbins online again recently – I wanted to take a close look at how he does what he does, because he just does such a great job of it. His language, for example, is sensational. His use of NLP (neuro linguistic programming) is beautiful. His way of connecting through the camera is awe-inspiring.

But all of what he *does* matters less than how he *thinks*.

This is a man who is always 'on'. I was at a training with him once, and he said he wrote *Awaken the Giant Within* in two weeks while he was training participants. I never complained about what I could accomplish within a short timeframe again.

Gary Player, the famous South African golfer, said that the more he practiced, the luckier he got. I find that the more success I have, the luckier I seem to get.

It really seems to be that luck happens with the more decisions you make, the more you have a go and the more you show up.

People can't believe how well we've done at The Coaching Institute in such a short time. Yet, to me, it seems ages. It's all perception, and given it's all made up, I'd rather have the view that it happens fast, it happens easily, and it happens for me all the time.

The only thing I believe that separates me from those struggling in business are the decisions I make on a regular basis to move me forward, despite circumstances.

I'm not interested in working with dreamers, schemers or scammers. They are looking for shortcuts and magic bullets and are constantly letting themselves (and others) down.

I'm only interested in people who are curious about how to get the results they want faster than what most people would have thought possible. And I know that they can do so simply because they will use the strategies that work, and will keep going, even in the face of adversity.

Not too long ago, it was considered normal to work until 60, retire and be bored – and then … die.

Unless you have been living in a cave, you will have realised that the days of conforming to such narrow definitions of work are long gone. These days we get to shape our futures the way we want them to be.

So here's the thing you now need to decide: are you prepared to do whatever is required to change your limited beliefs about money, to learn different ways of making money, and then to go out and make the stuff?

This is where you really do need to be honest with yourself. You see, what we are dealing with here is your mindset. I want you to change yours from whatever it is right now to that of a millionaire. Remember, as you are dealing with your mind, you won't be able to fool yourself. When it comes to your own mind, that's something you have to live with. It's also something you can't hide from. If you really, deep down inside believe you can't (or won't) change your mindset, then by pretending that you will just won't cut it. Do you get that?

And one other thing: deciding to change is just as easy as deciding not to change. You see, it takes the same amount of effort *to choose* either way. Choosing to choose is still a choice. So too is choosing not to choose.

Here's the good news... I believe every million made after the first is the easiest.

It's a challenge to make the first million, I'll give you that. It takes *focus, commitment* and *hard work*. But that doesn't mean it's impossible to get things going in the right direction before momentum kicks in.

Think of it this way: imagine the energy and the commitment it takes to get the Space Shuttle off the ground. I've heard that you can't get within miles of the launch pad because of the noxious fumes generated from the enormous amount of energy consumed in sending that craft into outer space. Yet, once the engines are jettisoned and the shuttle is in orbit, it's a different story. That massive weight travelling at 44,000 km/h can be manoeuvred with amazing ease. I'm told that if it was possible to tie a string to the shuttle's nose, you could simply alter its direction by tugging that string. Isn't that incredible? That is the advantage of total weightlessness.

So the effort that's required to propel it at 44,000 km/h while in orbit is, what? Nil, nothing – it's negligible. The maintenance crews on the ground keep tabs on things to make sure all systems are working as planned. This sounds more like a business than a machine, doesn't it?

So yes, as a business owner you do have to work hard in the beginning. At launch stage, it's no walk in the park. The idea is to push through the tougher stuff so you can get to the place where you don't have to work quite as hard, where you don't have to do everything but you get to enjoy the fruits of your efforts.

It's fear that holds you back. I think that, as I take my last breath, it won't be the things I failed at that I would regret the most, but the things I never tried.

The overwhelming regret most people have in the latter years of their lives is not what they did, but what they didn't do. So, if you are one of the many who feel constrained from doing what you really want to do, the best way I know of busting through your limits is getting the right education, goal setting, following through and accountability.

Change your thinking and your world has to change

I have made a big effort to make sure I hang out with the people who think positively about what they can accomplish. I don't spend time with people who whinge and complain about how hard it is.

I've also made sure I've got the education I needed. Wealth has a language. Making money has a language. I have learned that if I can 'language' it, I can have it. So a huge part of my earnings in my first few years went towards educating me on wealth, business and finance. I have invested, for example, over $250,000 on learning everything I can on marketing strategies that work. I have earned back that investment many times over.

The other thing I've done is to focus on where it is I want to be, and I imagine it's a reality for me right now.

To have what you want in life, be it a car, a house or the lifestyle of your dreams, you must first be able to see (or imagine) it. Once you can see it, then you need to believe that you already have it. In NLP, it's called 'acting as if'.

For instance, if you want to be a successful entrepreneur, you have to believe that you are already one. Once you believe this, your mind will simply accept this as a fact and behave accordingly. Your RAS – Reticular Activating System plays a vital part in your ability to achieve goals.

This is your Super Power.

Imagine you're at a party and there's noise and talking and music... Think of all the distractions. How much of this noise is brought to your attention? Very little. You can hear the general background noise, but most of us don't bother to listen to each of the individual sounds.

But then you hear someone across the room say your name. Suddenly your attention is full on. Your RAS is the automatic mechanism inside your brain that is going to bring relevant information to your attention.

It's the filter between your conscious mind and your unconscious mind. It takes instructions from your conscious mind and passes them along to your unconscious. In this example, 'listen for my name'.

You can deliberately program the reticular activating system by choosing the exact messages you send from your conscious mind.

You can set goals, or say affirmations, or visualise your goals. Napoleon Hill said that we can achieve any realistic goal if we keep on thinking of that goal, and stop thinking any negative thoughts about it. Of course, the reverse is also true. Keep thinking about how you'll never attain a goal, and that's what's going to happen.

Interestingly, your RAS can't distinguish between 'real events' and 'synthetic' reality. In other words, it tends to believe whatever message you give it.

Imagine that you're going to be shooting baskets in an upcoming basketball game. You can practice shooting the hoops by visualising it in your mind. This 'pretend' practice should improve your ability to shoot the hoops on game day.

So what I have learned to do it to create a very specific picture of my goal in my conscious mind. The RAS will then pass this on to my unconscious – which will then help me achieve the goal.

It does this by bringing to your attention all the relevant information which otherwise might have remained as 'background noise'.

Picture this – you are educated on wealth creation, on business and on marketing. Your language has changed so that the only way you know to talk about or think about your business is in terms of wealth, business or marketing principles that work.

Your language, your mindset and your RAS are all focused on the world you have created through educating yourself. Others start to pick up on this. They notice your confidence, your assertiveness and your decisiveness, and want to work with you, joint venture with you and do business with you.

Your clients become a better quality of person. Bad debts go down. People who rave about you start appearing.

You have a value-based business and the clients are coming to you.

Yes, it may be a bit of a challenge to start with, because it's not what we're seeing around us. We go to the office, and the phone isn't ringing. There's complaints, not raving fans. It's hard work. Remember the rocket ship that gets free of gravity. It's tough in the beginning, but worth the persistence.

In the beginning be mindful if you focus more on what you don't want. This doesn't mean blindly ignoring problems. This isn't 'positive thinking' our way to success. That's nonsense.

It's doing what needs to be done today, right now to correct the problems in your business, and at the same time getting the education you need so that your access to solutions grows day by day, until the existing problems are a thing of the past.

The problems won't go away. You'll always have problems, you'll just have a better quality problem.

I am convinced that success is possible if we find models of that success, get educated in what they do, do what we learn and keep moving towards our goals, regardless of the obstacles.

4

How to plan for business success

Action without planning is the cause of all failure.
Action with planning is the cause of all success.

BRIAN TRACY

How to get the business cranking

Once you understand the role played by your mindset in living life on your terms, then you'll understand the need to have a very clear mental picture of the type of life you want to lead before you can set about aiming to achieve it.

There's an urban legend that could be true that says that when people crash their cars they will find the only tree that's on the side of the road. It's like they seek out the only target that's there.

It's the same for learner drives. They're told to avoid the witch's hat, but what happens? The driver hits the witch's hat.

A friend of mine went on a driver training course. The trainer told him to not look at the cement walls of the race track, but to look at the road. Especially when they went into a skid. It took four times of the trainer physically twisting my friend's head back to the track and away from the cement walls for it to stick.

And each time my friend looked at the cement wall, that's where the car would start heading.

This is a great metaphor for what can happen when we want to create wealth. We can be working towards achieving a particular goal, and then notice an obstacle or a challenge. Instead of remaining focused on the goal, we shift our focus to the obstacle. In life, like with the driving course, what you focus on is what you move towards.

Imagine you're aiming to get your business online. You're doing the right things, making some progress – then you seem to plateau and, no matter what you do, you can't work out what to do next. The going definitely seems to be getting tougher than it had been when you started; some of the fun of the new stuff you're learning starts to fade and, frankly, it's getting tough to say 'no' to the other things you could be doing that are easier.

You tell yourself you've done pretty well, or that it's okay to not have the website completely up, given how hard you're tried, what with your workload and the kids to look after.

You give up the dream because you rationalise your lack of success. You make it okay to settle for the poor results you were getting. Again.

We do this all the time. Think about a time you wanted a pay an improvement in your business. You didn't get what you wanted in the timeframe you set for yourself. You're not even aware of it, but you rationalised your lack of results.

And so it goes on. You rationalise yourself into mediocrity until the next cycle of pain hits and you have to act. You take a few steps, get results, notice a plateau and the going begins to get a little tougher – and the rationalisation starts again.

The problem with this strategy is that each time we do it, we shave a little more off our self-esteem. We trade in our self-belief for settling. We drop our standards because we don't want to be disappointed the next time round. This is what most people do in life. *BUT*, now that you know what is actually happening with this specific approach and can recognise it, you can implement Plan B.

Plan B is simple. When you hit the plateau, you raise you standards. You ask more of yourself than you normally would, and you ask more of yourself than those around you would.

You don't settle: you step up.

It sounds so ridiculously simple that you're probably questioning if it is worth the investment or effort. Let me tell you it is.

Most people experience a setback and give up. But understand this: people who live their ultimate vision for life don't give up. They keep going even harder. They focus on where they are going to and not on what is holding them back.

I call it 'turning up after 3pm'. I can't remember who told me this, but there's a mentor who tells his clients that even if he turned up to teach the most advanced stuff he knew, most people would turn off, get tired, get bored, get confused or just give up by 3pm. He estimated that there would be 1 of 100 people still sticking at it by 3pm.

What I take from this is that I HAVE to turn up, alert and ready for action, at 3pm. Because that's when everyone else is turning off. I don't want to get the results that everyone else is getting. 'Everyone' is getting pretty ordinary results. I want extraordinary results, so I do what most people won't do or don't believe they can do.

I zig when everyone else zags. The fastest way to results is to see what the majority of people are doing and do something else – often the complete opposite.

Right, so what is the most effective way to go about this?

Begin with the end in mind

In business, or when engaged in a business conversation, I always start with the end in mind.

When someone asks for my opinion on something, they invariably just start talking, and I don't know what part of what they're saying to pay attention to. I stop them and say, "What is it you want help with specifically? What do you want to achieve as a result of this conversation?" I need to help that person focus what they're saying so they only communicate to me that which I need in order to answer their question.

The same is true in other situations. Take building a business for example. Before I even consider building my business, I must be able to visualise (or articulate) a clear and concise picture of what the business will look like when I am finished building it.

Too many people concentrate on the 'process' – they don't know why they do it; they do it just because they always have. Recently, I was chatting with one of my team members about a speech she needed to give, and she wanted me to help her on how to reduce its content.

But how could I help her unless I knew what results she wanted to achieve?

The whole conversation changed completely as a result of her getting clear on the outcome she wanted to achieve.

So how about writing down your end goal – and then working back from there? This will always keep you on track. If what you're doing isn't leading towards that end result, stop doing it.

I delegate my weaknesses as fast as possible. This includes things like bookkeeping, administration, ironing and cooking – I delegate these fast. You see, tasks go if they don't directly contribute to my goals.

When delegating, it is important to understand that the people you delegate tasks to are responsible for their completion – to the outcomes you set for them. Remember, too, that there are core tasks and non-core tasks; non-core tasks are delegated simply to get the process done by others. This contributes rapidly in dollar terms, because you are now free to focus on your strengths to get the bigger outcomes you want.

So how do you go about implementing this? How do you begin with the end in mind? Here's my simple process:

1. How do you see your business in three to five years? Outline your ideal outcome in detail.

2. What two or three great ideas can you actively implement for your business right now that will multiply your profits?

3. What do you need to stop doing that is preventing you achieving your ideal business?

4. What education do you need to make it as easy and enjoyable as possible to achieve your ideal business?

5. How much money does your business need to make to fund your lifestyle? What is your exit strategy?

Prepare a full set of plans

Once you have a good idea of what your business is going to look like **when you have finished building it**, it's time to begin the process of developing a full set of plans.

Planning is an indispensable part of any business. I know that most business owners neglect this part of the business process but, believe me, they do so at their own peril. I'm convinced that this is one of the reasons so many businesses fail during the first few years of their existence.

Most business owners don't plan to fail; they simply fail to plan.

I aim to be five times more prepared than I need to be for everything in business – meetings, chats, classes, negotiations, what I need to do to improve my business, everything.

You need to take aim, then walk backwards from there and plan out what has to happen.

Prioritise, delegate fast, and do what needs to be done. In our business, we call it the three Ds: Delegate it, Design it or Do it.

Delegate whatever is not your core function; design a system so someone else can do it next time; do it yourself if it needs to get done right now.

General George Patton, a US general who was famous for his leadership, even though he was a little outspoken once said, "Never tell people how to do things. Tell them what to do, and they will surprise you with their ingenuity."

Once you are comfortable with the reason for planning, it's time to get serious about setting some goals. You need to identify major milestones that will help get your business, and you, from where you are today to that point where you will be able to sit back and say, "I have completed building my business".

Goals

> Set priorities for your goals. A major part of successful living lies in the ability to put first things first. Indeed, the reason most major goals are not achieved is that we spend our time doing second things first ...
>
> ROBERT J. MCKAIN

This puts the reason for having goals in a nutshell. It clearly highlights one of the major uses of a goal's list. And it hints at another important aspect that you simply have to take on board: they need to be written down.

It's no good having all your goals piled up in your head. Forget it. There is plenty of evidence that the only goals worth having are those in a tangible form — on paper.

This section of the book is for you to record and update your vision as well as your long-term and short-term goals. It will provide you with a way to track how you are progressing throughout the next 12 months. It will help keep you focused and on track.

Use this as a workbook by filling in the blank spaces, or download the relevant pages at:

www.smallbusinessmastermindclub.com.au/business-success

and use them as a separate work book if you prefer. The important thing is that you implement a goal sheet upon which you record your progress.

What is my vision for my business?

How do I see myself adding value to my client's experience?

What's my ideal average business day? What happens? Who's there? How do I spend my time?

What I will achieve within the next 12 months? (Example)

Income: per year $_____

              per month $_____

              per week $_____

              per speaking event $_____

              average $ amount per client $_____

Ideal clients:

_____

Number of clients: _____

Hours worked IN the business to achieve this: _____

Which day do I set aside to work ON my business? _____

My ideal business (describe in detail how you imagine it to be):

_____

_____

_____

_____

_____

_____

The characteristics I need to bring to achieve these goals: (Example)

What stuff I need to quit right now?
My beliefs
Who I now hang out with?
Who I need to minimise my time with?
Who will be my role models?
Hours invested each week in education

My one-year goals (Example)

I earn:
I live:
I am with:
I enjoy:
I have let go of:
I invest my time in:
I feel passion for:
The emotions I choose are:
I choose:
I do:
I inspire:

My business one-year goals (Example)

It is: (insert date)
My business stands for: (what makes it something you're proud of?)
My business serves: (who are your ideal clients?)

90-day goals to achieve one-year business goals quarter #1 (Example)

1	Learn value-based marketing well enough to have boosted profit by 50%
2	Developed a sales system that boosts conversions by 5%
3	Designed and implemented three systems to improve collections and bad debt management
4	Hired a PA part time to assist with non-core
5	Hired a part time book keeper to manage the daily invoicing and collections
6	Launched new website using value-based marketing
7	
8	

Weekly task sheet to achieve your 90-day goals (Example)

Tasks to be completed in the next 7 days, 2 weeks or 1 month	Date completed
Studied this book	
Downloaded the free stuff to get more distinctions	
Planned out my website based on value-based marketing	
Advertised for a part time PA	
Advertised for a part time book keeper	
Designed one collections system	

Once you have completed this planning stage, it'll be time to seriously put your mind to finding yourself a great mentor.

Bonus material:

You can download the
**templates for goal setting and
business planning**
for free at:

THE COACHING

INSTITUTE

www.smallbusinessmastermindclub.com.au/business-success

5

How to get there faster and easier (driving a Ferrari)

People seldom improve when they have no other model
but themselves to copy.

OLIVER GOLDSMITH

So many people choose to learn what they need to by doing it, messing it up, and then doing it some more – all without asking for help or getting training, education or mentoring to learn how to do it faster or easier.

Traditionally, this has been called 'getting experience'. And as Barry LePatner says, good judgement comes from experience, and experience comes from bad judgement.

It makes no sense to learn the hard way when someone else could save you heaps of time and effort and get you there quicker and easier. What happens is that people who do it the hard way will often get tired, decide it's too hard and then quit. For them, getting to their goal seems to involve unacceptable sacrifices.

The easiest way to achieve success in anything is to find someone who has already done it, knows how to do it and can communicate easily and well how they did it. Modelling is the easiest way I know to get the results I want.

No matter what the investment, it's cheaper than learning the hard way.

When your business is building and things are happening, you don't have time to learn it all from scratch. It makes sense to find someone who's already done it, because they've invested in the years required to get great at it – which means you don't have to.

Edward Demming said that 95% of failure is the failure to follow a proven system. I have invested $125,000 in my education in the past 12 months, and have already earned $900,000 return on that investment. It would have taken me years to have learned this if I just relied on my own research – I shortcut my learning process and results by hiring mentors who already knew their stuff.

Want to know how much I invest in my own personal development each year? I invest a minimum of $50,000, and I always get a return far greater than that. So it makes sense to keep doing it, doesn't it? I get 'luckier' the more I learn and apply.

In seeking mentors, there are people who *do teach*, and people who *can teach*. This is not always the same thing. Buyer beware – take responsibility for your choice. Don't just model yourself on whoever is closest to you or whoever has the loudest voice. Seek the message that resonates with you and make sure the messenger already has the results they speak about.

A friend mine, Joe Pane, a coach and mentor to many, tells the story of how he finds mentors. It's two questions: Who are you? And, What have you done?

How to choose a mentor

It's vital that you select the right person for advice and guidance. It still staggers me the number of business owners I meet who tell me, with a straight face, that they always ask their neighbour, friend, father, mother, partner, whatever, when needing advice about some aspect of their business.

Now, this would be fine if the person they consulted was already a great business leader. Why people do this is really beyond me, and it really doesn't surprise me when it turns out that they end up getting the same results as the person they 'consulted' gets – nothing.

Would you, in all honesty, ask a painter about a problem you were experiencing with your heating system? Of course not. Then why would you ask your partner if you should be investing $25,000 in a training program on marketing and business skills and expect an appropriate and well-reasoned reply?

Would you expect your grocer to give you an expert opinion about whether you need root canal treatment on that nagging tooth?

You get my point.

The challenge you face now that you have decided you need to find a properly qualified mentor is this: how do you find such a person? How would you even know a good one from a mediocre one should you come across someone you thought would fit the bill?

The answer is that, like anything in business, you need to do your homework and prepare yourself. But as I have been saying, there's no need for you to reinvent the wheel here – just follow what those who have done this before have done. This is what I suggest:

1. Write down the qualities you need the most in your chosen mentor.

2. Write a list of potential mentors or business masters that you admire.

3. Research (online) mentors who offers services in the exact area you want assistance

4. Check out what they have accomplished

5. Opt in to their offers and see what they deliver to you for free

6. Get familiar with what they focus on, what they consider important and what they talk about – if it's not marketing, sales and leadership, move on

7. Create a list of questions you want answered. For instance:
   - How did they get started?
   - How much time do they spend on their business? Compared to 'in' their business?
   - How much time do they spend on personal development?
   - Did they buy their business or start it from scratch?
   - What makes them successful compared to other people?
   - How do they make decisions?

- How much do they delegate?
- What do they see as their responsibility?
- What do they think they must be great at?
- Who motivates and drives them?
- What unique marketing strategies do they use?

Modelling

I tell people that rather than inventing the wheel, find someone who drives a Ferrari and model that wheel.

I don't mean this literally. But the analogy is perfect.

Modelling is finding someone who has the results you want, then finding out everything you can about how they make decisions. When I find someone whose results I want, I search for the following:

- What's their philosophy of business? What do they see the reason for business as being? Where do they focus their time and attention?

- What business systems do they use? Is it value-based marketing? Is it something else?

- What are all the steps to their model? Break down each step in as much detail as you can.

- How do they think about business? Are they intense? Relaxed? Focused? There's no right or wrong, I just like to know what approach they use to get the results they get.

- How does what they do apply to my business? What parts of their systems can I adopt to boost our results?

- What is unique about what they do and how they do it? What stands out as different to the other people in the same business arena? How does that uniqueness work for them? Can I adopt it?

- What else is useful about what they do? What did they study? Where do they get their answers from? What are they reading?

I have studied with over ten mentors in the past 8 years, and learned so much from each of them. Each brought something different, that was appropriate to where I was at in my business at the time.

I don't question what they do as a sceptic. If they get results that are better than mine, and they have skills I don't have to make that happen, then I make sure I shut up, learn, apply, and get those same results.

I'm easy to mentor. I make it a point to be great at modelling, because it shaves literally decades off the time it would have taken to get the results we get.

Bonus material:

For a full checklist of what you want to see in a business you can download my own checklist for free at:

THE COACHING

INSTITUTE

www.smallbusinessmastermindclub.com.au/business-success

6

What makes a leader? Nine steps to leadership success

Do not follow where the path may lead. Go instead where there is no path and leave a trail.

RALPH WALDO EMERSON

In business, as with anything in life, there are basically two ways – and only two – of doing things: you can be proactive and take charge of the situation; or you can be reactive and respond to situations as they occur.

I prefer the first way.

After all, the major reason I prefer being in business for myself rather than being an employee is that I get to choose how things are done. I get to choose the lifestyle I lead, and I get to choose at what level I play the game of business.

One reason some don't survive in business is because they failed to take leadership seriously. They were content to be in business for themselves, but with the mindset of an employee. That simply doesn't work. If you're not leading the way, then who is? Your competitors? Your customers? Your suppliers? Your team? Nobody?

Many business owners overlook the whole topic of leadership and decide that they'll 'figure it out' as they go along. It's hit and miss, at best, and if it's anything like it was for me in the early days, it's tough!

I was too soft. Then I was way too hard. Then I was too friendly. Then

I was too 'stand-offish'. Then I thought it was all just not worth the effort. I drove myself nuts trying to crack the code on what it meant to be an effective leader.

Think of it this way. Your business is an entity in its own right. And if it survives (or has survived) those dangerous early years, then you'll know that it can assume a life of its own.

You need to lead your business or it will lead you.

So what do I mean by this? It means you have to be an intelligent leader. You need to have LQ: leadership intelligence™.

Consider this for a moment. Your business can do nothing by itself. Take away the human element, and what have you got? Nothing. Just an entity, that's all.

So you have to decide to steer it in a certain direction, to give it a personality (think culture), and to develop an image for it in YOUR CHOSEN marketplace (think personality).

In short, you have to assume the role of the leader.

So what actually IS a good leader? How do you know WHAT a good leader's role is in any business?

Step one: Stay on message

A leader must always focus on what is core for the business. By core, I mean what you do best and what the market knows you for. Don't go off core because something else looks shiny and new; stay with core until the core is a machine that can run itself.

Always start with the end in mind – always have purposeful conversations. Start with, "Why are we having this conversation?", and "Why are we focusing on this, doing this, designing this?"

All conversations and actions should move your business closer to achieving its purpose. For example, your first choice could be to get a mentor to guide you to achieve better results.

These are priorities I have had in my business since the beginning:

- I always have at least one mentor

- I always stay true to core – even with lots of new opportunities,

I improve what makes the most money, before anything else

- I focus every day on sales
- I focus every day on marketing
- I am always looking for ways to generate new and better quality leads
- I never take my eyes off the money – the profit and loss, the bad debts, the management of the cash flow

Leadership is about saying what you mean and meaning what you say. Question first why something is being focused on, and whether you agree it will move you and your business towards its purpose – then continue. If it won't move the business towards its purpose, then change the actions.

When something occurs, then:

- do it (if it's a one-off and can't be delegated)
- design a system to deal with it (if that's possible)
- delegate both (if you can)

Be calm, no matter what is happening. People want guidance, especially when they're stressed; you mustn't add to their stress by being stressed yourself. You may go nuts inside, but always look calm and sound calm, whatever you do.

New leaders tend to either hold on too tightly and be overly dictatorial, or be way too friendly. Don't be friends: don't be a dictator. Instead, start out being a leader who is action-focused – in the beginning, do as much as you can to demonstrate your competence. This will build trust.

Once trust has been established, become an inspirational leader so you don't have to do the thing to inspire; it's enough that you have spoken about it – your team will do it because they respect you as a leader.

Step two: Use a leadership model that works

Use the TACOCA model for management. It's an acronym formed from the words:

- Trust
- Agenda
- Challenges
- Opportunities
- Commitment
- Accountability

Let me explain how this works.

Step three: Trust

Trust is built through saying what you mean and meaning what you say.

Part of building this is having the right people around you. Understand the DISC analysis of the members of your team. We place and manage people according to their DISC personality profiles so they can succeed and we know how to support them.

For example, someone who is high 'C' (compliant) should be placed in a highly systemised role where they will know what to do next, or where they can design the system to help with what happens next. You should manage them with a calm voice, and conversations should focus on what is within their control and influence or they'll stress.

If someone is an 'S' (steady), place them into a role where long-term relationships are important, and focus conversations around who could be involved that they can rely on, as they apply systems.

If, on the other hand, a team member is an 'I' (influential), they could work in sales. Hire the 'collaborator I', rather than the 'peacock I', as you want the person to focus less on themselves and more on how they relate to others.

We hire 'C's for administration roles; we hire 'S' personalities for client relationship roles; we hire 'I' types for sales. I'm a 'D' (dominant), but I don't lead with 'D' and talk in 'D' as this is way too confronting and direct; I talk in a quiet tone but, internally, as a leader, I am always in 'D' mode – determined, single-focused; nothing will get in my way.

It's important to have a 'D' as a leader so you can have the determination to push through obstacles, but it's important to manage each person in their preferred style and not yours.

Step four: Agenda

This is about knowing what our purpose is for doing something or talking about it. As a leader, you must always be clear on the desired outcome.

Conversations always start here, because if you know the end you desire, you then know how to have a targeted conversation. Start the conversation with, 'What is it we want to accomplish today?' or "What are we looking to achieve?"

Step five: Challenges

This is where you discuss what obstacles you need to anticipate when looking at a new goal. For example, if you want to prepare for an event, the potential challenges include getting a hotel conference room that suits your needs, and getting support from the hotel staff. So, to manage these challenges, you would do your research on what you ideally want; then write a system and operations manual for your needs so that, moving forward, you always know the blueprint for what you prefer in a hotel conference room.

The other challenges are the internal ones: what do the team members see as getting in their way? Lack of confidence? Lack of competence? Do they see obstacles ahead that stop them being able to get started?

It's not a lack of desire that stops someone doing something; it's the challenges they perceive that they don't know how to overcome. This is why I am patient when things are not actioned.

It's about helping team members confront their fears and talking about potential challenges. Revisiting what's needed helps. Talk about their abilities, the importance of learning new things to succeed personally – then ask for a deadline of action in that area of perceived difficulty.

The third way I look at challenges when an agenda is set (for example to design a new payment system for the business), is from the problems perspective.

I ask three questions: "What could go wrong with this?" and "Where will this not work" and "What else will this impact?"

These questions mean I am constantly anticipating consequences. For example, changing a payment system will impact: the sales team, how we market, what we mail to prospects, what happens at events, students who are already on the original system...

I continually look for potential risks and weaknesses in new ideas. I know this sounds negative, but it's not; it's being prepared and able to anticipate what could go wrong and planning accordingly. For example, a new payment system was looked at, and by asking this question we were able to anticipate that students may find it difficult to adjust to the change, so we put together a fact sheet to make it easier.

Step six: Opportunities

This is about focusing on the potential choices we have available to us. What could we do if there were no barriers?

It's called 'Disney World', and it's about not knocking any idea, no matter what it is; it's about exploring all that we could do, rather than all that we should do.

It's about free thinking, brainstorming and anything goes. It's important to let any idea come, because bad ideas lead to great ideas, which leads to something never thought of before.

This brainstorming is how we came to offer the Mastermind Program. It started out as 'how do we give our students even more value?' We 'Disneyed' this question and came up with dozens of ideas. The idea to provide a program that focused on marketing and not coaching looked like a bad idea at first, because it didn't seem core to our business. But then we realised it was core, because it was a skill-set vital to any new business owner's success.

Opportunities that aren't core have to wait until the core is done so well it could run itself. We don't make any decisions to expand until we can deliver the core of our business effortlessly. Non-core ideas, like going to another city, occur once core is solid and the expansion won't put our resources under too much stress.

This can slow you down and frustrate you as a leader – but it's about taking care of the clients first, before you expand into new markets or locations.

Step seven: Commitment

Let me give you an example from my business. Once we knew the outcome we wanted, we brainstormed about how to improve our turnaround time on emails. We explored what could prevent this happening – difficult questions only a few people could answer, so it falls to them. And then we looked at the opportunities: more training for other team members so the load could be spread. We then committed to the action that was best.

In this example, we started a FAQ section in the ops manual so newer team members could have access to the answers to the harder questions – this way, everyone could handle the questions, not just a select few.

This became the agreed path – this is the commitment phase of the conversation.

Once this was done, all that was left was accountability.

Step eight: Accountability

When will this be done by? If it's an ongoing project, what milestones need to be achieved? How will we know this is done?

The whole system is done using 90-day plans.

Each 90-day period, all team members establish what they will accomplish in the next quarter. The goals could be part of their own personal development as well as goals that move the business closer to its objectives.

There are six outcomes per team member so, by the end of each quarter, massive inroads will have been made to move the business forward, and everyone will have a sense of achievement.

The outcomes for someone in student support might look like this:

Student Support: Jack Smith July 1st to Sept 30th		
Outcomes:	Assistance needed	Completed
FAQ's done and circulated	Student Support manager	
New website for members uploaded with content	Techie	
All events run smoothly and according to operations manuals	Events coordinator	
Assessors receive feedback in real time on new assessment system		
New manual created and printed ready for end of year training	Printer	
Student awards night ready to go in Nov	Whole team	

Then, each week, tasks are set that will ensure the achievement of these outcomes. These tasks are smaller steps towards the outcomes.

The above is an example of starting with the end in mind, and helps team members know what they are focusing on.

Tasks for the week would be:

Task	Done
Collect emails and answers of hard questions and compile into one file	
Meet with Student Support Manager for info on what types of templates need to be uploaded onto the new website	
Review the next quarter of events and place tasks into the calendar	
Review new assessment system to ensure it works	
Book time with printer for new manual discussion	
Discuss with team at next cultural lunch day what they want to see at the awards night to make it special	

While this wouldn't be all the student support team member would do for the week, these are the minimum things that need to be done, and all need to be ticked by the time of the next meeting.

Step nine: Developing the team

Depending on their self-leadership abilities, leaders may:

- tell them what to write in the task list
- discuss what goes in and then confirm recommendations
- ask questions and let the team member set the tasks
- or let the team member do it themselves and get on with it

When someone starts out in our business, they start with getting strong direction, because while their confidence may be high, their competence is low, regardless of what they think; they don't have all the facts.

Direction reduces as skills and competence improves and there is evidence of their ability to take into account all that needs to be considered.

The next part of my leadership style is what I like to call 'criteria for success'. I deal with facts, rather than how something feels to me. So, for every decision being made, I want to know what the criteria are for making the decision. For example, when deciding on a new marketing brochure, it's not about the thing being 'pretty' – it's rather about what needs to be there based on the evidence we have of what works.

We know that testimonials work, examples work, pictures work, and guarantees work. So given that these are known to help the marketing succeed, those things go into the brochure.

If we're not sure what else is critical for success, we get educated.

To put our last brochure together, I studied brochures for a year. I was looking for the elements that worked; ones that people could demonstrate had been successful. The brochure was assembled based on these criteria – not on what I thought looked good, or I was personally proud of. You see, it's not about me; it's only about what gets the result.

You are responsible

The hallmark of a great leader is the characteristic of responsibility – for themselves, their business and their achievements and failures. And by responsibility, I mean 100% responsibility.

Successful people don't look for excuses as to why something didn't turn out as expected. They know that when it comes to that most hallowed of concepts, success doesn't depend on anyone else but themselves. So forget about blaming the economy, your product, your clients or the weather; none of them matter when it comes to success. Remember: great fortunes are made whenever there is an economic downturn; great business leaders emerge from poverty; must-have products spring up from fleeting ideas.

Understand that you alone are responsible for your thoughts and actions. You alone get to decide what you want to do, when you want to do it, and how you want to do it. And it is from actions, not thoughts, that things happen.

The world must go on, regardless of the state of the economy. People must eat, drink, get about and entertain themselves. Money has to circulate. The only question is, what part do you want to play in all of this? Are you content just sitting on the sidelines waiting for others to do something, or will you take action? Are you a responsible leader? Do you have leadership intelligence? Can you lead, motivate and inspire your team, or will you sit back and allow the general chitchat of the workplace affect the culture of your business? Have you already lost control, or are you still in control? The choice is yours – which one will it be?

Your role as a business leader

As a business leader, you are the one others will be looking up to. Are you up to the task?

Do you have what it takes to lead? If you're not sure what this means, don't worry – leadership can be learned. It may be something some people are born with, but it really is just a state of mind. That means you can choose to be the leader.

Think about that for a moment.

Here are some key characteristics of a leader:

- 100% responsibility
- 100% accountability
- Clarity of vision
- Decisiveness
- Self-belief
- Confidence
- Takes action
- Persistence
- Stays focused
- Flexibility
- Open mindedness
- Continual education
- Motivation
- Enthusiasm
- Positive attitude
- Empathy

Don't be frightened by these. They are just some that spring to mind. There are probably many more, but the important thing to bear in mind is that this list is not complete or exhaustive. It is dependent of the situation, too; so don't think that just because you are a little short in self-belief, you can't make a good leader. That can and will change as you get runs on the board. The more successful you become, the more self-assured you will get. But start out in another market after conquering your existing one, and you'll probably find your level of self-belief plummets again. That's normal. Life is dynamic and constantly changing. Your job as a leader is to be proactive and in charge, not only of your business, but of yourself as well. And that is only a decision that needs to be taken.

Bonus material:

For a free copy of the
Leadership In Action Model
report go to:

www.smallbusinessmastermindclub.com.au/business-success

For more information, or to have yourself
and your team assesssed using the
DISC Profiling Tool
go to:

www.smallbusinessmastermindclub.com.au/business-success

PART II:

Your marketing system for massive success

7

Create instant expert status

You want a niche an inch wide and a mile deep.

UNKNOWN

What kind of business person are you? A generalist or a specialist?

So, what's the difference?

Generalists will always supply the background noise in the market. They will always clamour for work, wonder how to get it happening and feel overworked. They are technicians doing the hard labour of their craft. The specialists are the elite. Enough said.

A specialist is someone who has expertise in something. They are the opposite of the generalist, who is a jack-of-all-trades.

People and businesses that are perceived experts in their niche do much better than a person or business that is a little bit of everything.

A niche market is a focused, targetable portion of a market. By definition, then, a business that focuses on a niche market is addressing a need for a product or service that is not being addressed by mainstream providers.

You can think of a niche market as a narrowly defined group of potential customers. For instance, instead of offering cleaning services, a business might establish a niche market by specialising in blind cleaning services.

Every business I know who operates within a narrow niche has income that *far* exceeds that of the generalist providers (except Myer, but we don't have their budget!). After all, who would you rather see about a lump on your leg? A GP or the specialist for leg lumps? When you search online for a solution to your rose fungus, do you just type 'rose' into your search engine or do you type in 'rose fungus'?

I think we smaller operators are poised in a unique situation where we can create our business and our market. We are creating it all the time. I think BP or BHP are in different situations. They rely upon tens of thousands of people to do what they do and face the prospect of mines or oil rigs closing down – so the effect for them is far reaching if something goes wrong. But I think small business leaders are very lucky, as downscaling is not that difficult. It is fairly easy to do and the profits, as you know, are very high. Not only that, but the overheads are quite low in our sector of the economy (if we want them to be) and, as long as we stay innovative, we can face the economic challenges that lie ahead with confidence.

Assume you were the owner of a restaurant. How would you fill it with customers every evening? When I ask this question during seminars, typical answers I receive include: have a great chef; have beautiful ambiance; provide great service; make sure the food is fantastic.

None of them are right.

The number one way to fill a restaurant is to make sure you have a hungry hoard. If you have a starving crowd, they will fill your restaurant.

So, you can have the most beautiful brochures, and the most fabulous service; you can be the most talented business person in the world – but what must you have to build a really successful niche?

A market.

There must be a demand. Just because you are great at your calling and you are passionate about it, unless you've got masses of people who feel the same way and are into it as passionately as you are, then you're going to go hungry.

Criteria for choosing your niche

Criterion # 1: The potential clients have to have a problem.

A niche is any part of the market where the potential client has a specific problem they want solved. For us in our coach training market, the problem we solve very specifically is how to have life on your terms in your own coaching business.

In the Small Business Mastermind Club, the specific problem we solve is how to help small business owners boost profits and get their lives back through using value-based marketing.

Criterion #2: How much does the client desperately want your product?

In coming up with niches and products, ask yourself the question: does the customer lie awake at night worrying about a problem that your product would solve?

There is a big difference between a topic that people desperately want, and a topic that you think people need. People don't search for topics that you think they need. For example, last month, according to the Google keyword tool, only 49,500 people worldwide searched for 'household budget' – but 550,000 people searched for 'buy a TV'.

Products about 'prevention' are much harder to sell than products about 'cure'. For example, a book about how to prevent lung cancer won't sell nearly as well as a book about how to cure lung cancer. The first one is something that lots of people need, but the second one is something that people who are affected desperately want.

Criterion # 3: Is the topic an 'inch-wide, mile-deep' niche?

It seems to go against logic, but the more you narrow your niche, the more money you make. Here's an example of a niche being progressively narrowed:

- books
- writing books
- how to write books
- how to write nonfiction books

Once you have come up with an idea that seems interesting, you can use the Google keyword tool to find a niche within a niche (don't worry just yet about the details about Google keywords; I'll be discussing that in more detail shortly). To do this, put the keywords in order of search volume by clicking on 'Sorted by' and select Global Monthly Searches.

Then look for sub-niches.

For example, if you search for 'marketing', you'll see it has 151,000,000 searches per month. This is too broad a niche. But if you look down the list you'll see some great potential sub-niches. For example 'marketing management' (673,000 searches), 'web marketing' (673,000 searches), and 'small business marketing' (201,000 searches).

Criterion #4: They will spend money on the solution

If the potential client can get all the answers they need for free online, then there is little justification for going into that niche. Recipes are a great example of this. You can find pretty well any recipe for free online, so it's difficult to see why someone would pay for a recipe book online too.

To find out how much free information is there, again look at every site on the first page of a Google search on your top three key words for your chosen niche. This time, see how much free information there is that is the same as the information you will be providing.

If there is lots of free stuff, can you differentiate yourself? For example, there is lots of free information about report writing. However, a lot of it is difficult to make sense of, and there is absolutely nothing about a step by step process that makes it easy.

Compare this to life coach training, where there are plenty of well-written success stories, and lots of plain-English explanations of the profession, but to get training on life coaching for free is not easy to find. This niche meets all the criteria for success.

Criterion # 5: Number of people searching for your topic

You need to make sure you have enough volume in your chosen niche. That means that you need to have enough people (who lie awake at night desperately wanting a solution to their problem) looking for your key words.

Here are the numbers to use.

Some experts recommend to look for 2–3 key words around the topic with around 500,000–1,000,000 searches per month on Google.

I make millions in a niche where the search volume is the following:

- Life coach training 18,100

- Becoming a coach 12,100

- Become a life coach 9,900

Here's an example of a niche where I know a business makes tens of thousands of dollars a year:

- Skin cancer 823,000

- Melanoma 550,000

Criterion # 6: Number of Google ads

I also want the niche to have evidence that another one or two marketers are already in the niche. I don't like it when there is no one marketing in the niche, because it makes me think it's probably not attracting people who will spend money.

Go to Google and type in 'small business marketing success' as your key words and hit 'search'. You will see a bunch of websites listed down the left hand side of the page. You'll also see some ads on the right hand side of the page, and perhaps across the top of the page.

If you go online and type in coaching training, notice how down the right hand side there are quite a few businesses there. These are sponsored links, and businesses pay Google a fee each and every time someone clicks on any of the ads. This is called Pay Per Click advertising. It makes sense then that if there are a number of marketers there willing to spend money to be there, then they are probably making money.

Generally, the higher up the list of Google ads you are, the higher the click-through rate. It's a bit like an auction. The more you pay, the more you rank in the sponsored ads. I've noticed an increase over the years in what it costs to be there, but it's still the best targeted traffic source I can find fast and easily.

These are the 'sponsored' ads. Any business can get an ad there. Here's how it works.

Google ads work on a pay per click basis. That means that whenever someone types any one of your key words into a Google search, your ad appears on the right side of the screen. Google only charges you if someone clicks on your ad and goes to your website.

The position of your ad relative to other ads depends on three things:

1. The amount you pay per click. In general, the more you pay, the higher your ad will appear.

2. The click-through rate of your ad. If you write an ad that has a high click-through rate (because you've written a good headline and good sales copy on the following two lines), then Google will reward you by putting your ads higher on the list.

3. It's not confirmed (Google is very secretive about how it calculates what happens) but there is a view that you will rank higher in the adwords sponsored list if you also have a regular site that ranks well. For example, we rank on page one organically for www.thecoachinginstitute.com.au and we seem to rank higher for slightly less PPC fees in the sponsored search listings as a result of that.

If there are lots of ads (more than 20), you will struggle to get your ad in the top 10 for a reasonable price – at least initially, until you build enough volume. Since most people only look at the first page of a Google search, your ad will rarely be seen.

Here's how to find out how many competing ads you have on Google:

1. Go to Google and do a search on one of your top 2–3 key words. Count the number of ads (Google calls them sponsored links) you see on the first page. Make sure you count the ones in blue on the top left of the screen, as these are also paid ads. It's pretty common to have up to 11 or 12 on the first page.

2. Then click on the words *more sponsored links* if it appears at the bottom

of the list of ads on the right side of the screen. Count the number of ads that come up. Note though, that some ads show more than once, so be careful not to count them twice.

3. I also like to click through on these ads and see what the business does – if I arrive at a regular site that doesn't have a 'call to action' – ie it doesn't ask for my contact details in return for some cool free stuff, I discount them as potential competition. If there's lots of sites that offer free cool stuff for my details then I see it as a high competition niche.

If a topic has more than 20 Google ads, I would be very wary about continuing with it. However, there are exceptions. As I said before, if the other ads all lead to sites that are boring, don't offer free content for your contact details and are just shop windows, I will probably consider giving it a go. If you have a really good niche within a niche, and you can convey this in a three-line ad, then you should be able to get very targeted traffic to your site.

Targetted traffic means that more people who go to your site will probably buy your product. You have fewer tyre-kickers. If you can do this, then you can afford to pay more per click. However, this is quite an advanced strategy – I wouldn't be trying it as a first one.

Criterion # 7: Number of products for sale on the topic

You will quickly get used to recognising a good sales letter:

*   it is one with a grabbing headline
*   it will be structured as a long, one-page site
*   it will have very few graphics so it is quick to load up.
*   it will have a number of inducements to buy (bonuses, offers, guarantees, and testimonials)

You need to look at every site on the first page of a Google search on your top three key words for your chosen niche, and see if there is a good sales letter. Look at both the free side and the Google ads. If there is a few good sales letters, think carefully about whether you can compete. Is your product going to be significantly different? If not, can you change it enough to make it different?

I would tend to hesitate with a niche where there is already someone selling a product from a good sales letter, and where I am unable to differentiate sufficiently. I would also hesitate if there is a great site that has a fantastic free offer that is exactly what the market wants.

But that's not to say that I'd eliminate any idea that already had a market-match product being sold. Often it's possible to have 4–5 businesses selling really well all in the same niche, because they are all different enough that they don't compete. And if you've chosen a topic that people are passionate about, then they'll often buy more than one product on the same topic.

Profitable niches

Profitable niches are everywhere, and especially where there are hobbyists. People get really fired up about their hobbies and will pretty well buy anything they can find on their chosen passion.

Think about it... What's something you're 'into'? Did you buy just one thing on this passion or more than one thing? For me it's marketing. I didn't just buy one book. I have dozens of books. But I didn't stop there. I also bought the programs, the CD's, the DVD's and went to the courses. I am always looking out for the latest 'thing' on marketing to add to my collection.

Better than hobbyists is showing people how to monetise their hobby. Brett McFall, an internet marketer who knows nothing about scrap booking, often tells the story of how he has a successful site on making money scrap booking. You can check out the site here:

www.scrapbookingprofits.com

Go to:

www.wire-sculpture.com

and read through the sales letter. Daryl and Andrew Grant, Internet marketing success stories, talk about Preston Reuther, who owns this site. Preston makes wire jewellery and probably could have made a decent living selling what he made, but instead he sells a business system to people who are interested in turning wire jewellery making into their own home-based business.

Here's a great example of differentiating in a crowded niche. Go to:

www.yoga-teacher-training.org

and read through the sales letter.

This site makes thousands of dollars each month. Again, the owner of this business shows people how to make money from their hobby or passion.

Become an expert

Once you've identified your niche, the next thing that you need to do is become recognised as the expert in that niche. So how do you go about doing this?

Here's what I suggest:

1. Go to the library and pull out every book there is on your chosen niche.

2. Go online and download everything you can find on that niche.

3. Read it all – read the title, the contents page and the index at the back, the report. Listen to the CD's.

4. You're looking for information that will help the average person in that niche.

5. Ask yourself what would make your perfect clients flutter with joy. What is their most selfish desire? What would put them in heaven?

6. Then toss aside any book or online product that doesn't deliver exactly that.

7. Toss aside the joke books, the boring books, the fiction books, the photo books. Discard any online product that looks the same as everything else.

8. If the author isn't clear, toss the book.

9. Skim boring sections.

10. Start taking notes of the difference that makes the difference.

11. Note what appears to be unique information that most people won't know.

12. It takes less than one day to do this.

13. It's the information that makes you valuable.

14. The steps above prepare you for developing your product.

Keyword spying

Good business is all about taking charge and not being reactive. It is about being decisive and not leaving things to chance. It's about knowing what your target market thinks, does and wants.

So, how do you go about achieving this when developing your niche in the market?

The answer is to get a good handle on what your niche market looks for online.

How do you do this? Through monitoring keywords. I have found:

www.wordtracker.com

an excellent site that enables you to see how many people are searching for a particular word or phrase on the Internet. This can help you decide if your idea is a good one or not.

The cost to achieve this is only $365 a year, and it's research money well spent. 'Spent' is actually the wrong word, because I like to think of it as an investment in my business.

If no one is searching for the keywords you think of, those keywords are duds.

What you are aiming for when deciding on a niche for your business is one that gets lots of searches, but not so many that your prospective clients get lost in the clutter of other competitors.

You want high interest and low competition. High interest is 20,000 to 40,000 searches a month; low is two to three others in the same space.

Discussion groups and blogs

Another great way to find out what people are talking about is through on-line discussion groups and blogs. The easiest way to find discussion groups that fall within the general topic you are interested in is to visit

http://groups.google.com

Here you will be able to search for groups on just about any topic imaginable.

Clickbank

You can use Clickbank (the Internet's largest seller of eBooks) to find out how well different eBook topics are selling, because Clickbank ranks their eBooks by popularity. You can see which topics are selling well (and view the sales letter) by browsing through Clickbank's list of over 10,000 eBooks. To do this, go to

www.clickbank.com

and click the *buy products* tab. Choose a category to browse, (for instance 'Health products') to see a list of the top eBooks that are in that category.

The list is ranked according to the number of sales, so if you look at the ones at the top, you can see what's selling the best in that category. Then you can then narrow it down by clicking on the sub-categories (such as 'nutrition') to see the top eBooks in each of the sub-categories. If you click on the eBook title, it will take you to the sales page, where you can check out their sales copy, offers, guarantees, etc. Even if you don't sell that eBook, it's still really useful for research purposes.

Google

Another powerful tool you should use to research niche markets is Google's keyword tool. Type in

www.googlekeywordtool.com

This website gives you the number of Google searches per month that have been made on a particular word or phrase. By typing in any key words you want, you can find out how many searches are being made for that particular phrase or words. Generic terms like *how to, build, learn* or *buy*, will let you find the most common things that people want to build, learn or buy.

Before you start, make sure you change the 'location searched' to *all countries*, then type your keyword or phrase into the search box. Once you've done that, type in the security code provided, and click *get keyword ideas*.

If you scroll down, you'll see a list of the most common phrases that include these words. I suggest you put them in order of search volume by clicking on the heading *Approximate search volume.*

Test the market

Once you've arrived at what appears to be a viable niche for your business, you want to take the time to test whether it is viable or not. Successful business is all about testing and measuring what works and what doesn't. There are far too many examples of product launches that should have worked, but flopped simply because a seemingly obvious factor wasn't taken into account. Things like this get picked up through simple testing and measuring campaigns.

One of the things to consider is how many competitors there are in that niche.

Type in the key words or phrase and see how many ads appear down the right hand side as sponsored ads. Click on them and see if they are selling something, what the price is, what they're offering and what bonuses they have.

Check over the next week or so to see if they stay there. If they run a continuous campaign they are possibly making money from that niche.

Next you want to see how many sites are going to be in competition with you. If there are more than five or six sites doing a great job of selling into that niche, you could be going into a crowded market. If there are five or six sites and they don't look very good, (what this means is covered later) you could do well if you do better with your website.

Next you may want to set up an AdWords campaign to see if anyone visits a one-page test site that you've set up. It could, for instance, ask one question:

> "If we were to provide you with a series of classes that covers the ten top items of interest in a particular topic (here you tailor this to suit your niche market or area of interest), what would you want to know?"

If no one responds, it's a dud. If you get hits, it's a possible starter. If you get over 30 hits, you could have a product on your hands; you just don't know yet how much they will spend.

More hits, your idea probably has legs. You can produce something from this.

8

Your ideal client: the formula for constant repeat sales

Know your client.

FRANK KERN

Your ideal client

This is one of the most profitable conversations we could have. I know learning this and applying it has added at least one million of profit to my business, and I'm only just getting good at it.

Your avatar is – the ideal, average client you attract who does business with you, is happy to do business with you and sees you as an exact match for the problem they want solved.

They will stay with you, spend more money with you and like you because you deliver exactly what they want.

That's who you should always do business with.

BEFORE you can go to market you need to create a story, become a character, deliver great content and become their trusted adviser.

To do this, you need to know THEM.

- Who is your prospect? Write down a real description. Pretend they are sitting across from you. Try to nail down the average person, in terms of likes and dislikes, income, sex and age etc

- What is causing them pain?

- What's their biggest problem?

- What miracle would deliver their biggest desire whilst solving their biggest problem? It could be a product that holds their hands as the do the steps, or it could be someone else doing it for them. It could be the steps are given to them one at a time with help.

- What are their top fears and frustrations? What gets them mad? What gets them worried?

- What do they want? What is the outcome they are really after? The secret thing they want that isn't a result that's tangible, but a feeling or an experience?

- What are their top wants and desires based on what they actually say they want? What are they really after? How is that different to what they think they want?

- What does your XXX do or give your prospect that they doesn't know about? What are the hidden benefits that your prospect doesn't know about?

- How do they like to receive their goodies? Email? Membership? Mailed folders? Contact with people face-to-face? Contact with people on the phone? Networking?

- What forums do they go to? What do they write about?

- What are they afraid will be discovered about them? What do they want no one to know about them?

- What would happen for them if they got their desire?

- Finish this sentence for your prospect: "If I could just..."

- What's your prospect's name?

- If I could pick them out from a crowd, who am I looking for?

- What do they do for a living right now?

- What other identifying traits does this person have? Married? Kids? Past bankruptcy?

Now fill in the blanks for the next paragraph:

> Hi, <THEIR NAME>. I know it's not easy being a <THEIR AGE> year old <THEIR GENDER> and <THEIR IDENTI-FYING TRAIT> who's trying to <THEIR DESIRES OUT-COME>... especially when you're tied up most of the time working as a <THEIR JOB>. And when you think about <THEIR BIGGEST PROBLEM>, it can seem overwhelming. So I want to just take a minute and let you know everything is going to be fine. How can I say this? Because I know how you feel. Getting <THEIR DESIRED OUTCOME> wasn't easy for me either and I sure had challenges of my own... just like you do now.
>
> I remember... <HERE YOU'RE GOING TO TELL YOUR STORY, WHICH IS IN THE NEXT SECTION>...

So if Frank Kern (online marketing legend) was doing this exercise, writing to his prospect for a beginner's marketing product, he'd be writing to a 45 year old man named Bob who sells insurance. Bob is married with two kids who drive him nuts and his wife thinks he's an idiot for trying this internet stuff. He's about 10 kilo's overweight and wears glasses. He wears a short sleeved button down shirt (white) and khaki pants. His shoes are brown leather. His biggest desire is to make enough money to quit his job, which pays him $58,000 a year. His biggest problem is he doesn't know where to start and he gets information overload because he sees so many different promotions.

This is what Frank wrote about him using the above template:

> "Hi, Bob, it's Frank. I know it's not easy being a 45 year old dad trying to make it online AND juggle a family... especially when you're tied up most of the time selling insurance. And when you think about trying to piece all this stuff together and find a place to start, it can seem overwhelming. Especially since you're getting a new "make money" email every ten minutes. So I want to just take a

minute and let you know everything is going to be fine. How can I say this? Because I know how you feel? Making enough money online to quit my job wasn't easy for me either and I sure had challenges of my own... just like you do now. I remember when I was broke back in 1994. It was bad enough that I didn't have two nickels to rub together... but then a flood came through my home and all of my possessions. So then I was broke and homeless!

I'm lucky I didn't have my two kids to support back then because I don't know how I would have done it. And I'm really lucky I discovered the one little thing that would change my life forever. It's the one thing that's let me know I'll never have a job again and it's called..."

FROM "MASS CONTROL" BY FRANK KERN

Now let me have a go for The Coaching Institute avatar...

Hi, <JACQUI>. I know it's not easy being a <45> year old <MUM> and <JUGGLE A FAMILY> who's trying to <HAVE A LIFE OF REAL MEANING>... especially when you're tied up most of the time working as a <SCHOOL TEACHER>. And when you think about <HOW YOU'VE NEVER DONE ANYTHING LIKE THIS BEFORE>, it can seem overwhelming. So I want to just take a minute and let you know everything is going to be fine. How can I say this? Because I know how you feel. Getting <TO A PLACE WHERE YOU'RE WITH LIKE MINDED PEOPLE, CONTRIBUTING AND GROWING> wasn't easy for me either and I sure had challenges of my own... just like you do now.

I remember... <FEELING TRAPPED BY THE CHOICES I HAD ALREADY MADE, AND CONFUSED ABOUT HOW TO BUILD A LIFE OF AUTHENTICITY, ESPECIALLY WHEN I WAS SO BUSY JUST GETTING BY AND TAKING CARE OF WHAT I ALREADY HAD IN MY LIFE>...

Once you're clear on your avatar and everything about them, you then do all your marketing to them and only them. You answer questions that you get as if you are talking only to this avatar.

If you don't, you will have people buy your stuff who aren't your ideal average client, and they'll be disappointed with what they get, or you'll find it difficult to help them, because you've designed a program or delivered a product that is only for the avatar, and not for this other person.

If you do only talk to the avatar, regardless of who makes the inquiry, then you'll always be delivering 'on message' to the people who want exactly what you deliver.

You can't be all things to all people, and you never want to be.

You want to be one thing to one group of people, over and over again.

Bonus material:

For a complete
"Avatar Checklist"
go to:

www.smallbusinessmastermindclub.com.au/business-success

9

Being the character your dream client wants to do business with

People come to you to get content.... and they stay with you because they become attached to the character you portray.

FRANK KERN

Your character

Once you know your avatar BACKWARDS AND FORWARDS, you now need to become the character that would be most appealing for this avatar. Your goal is to become the expert leader who is looked to and trusted for great content and solutions.

The reality is, your market is going to follow someone. May as well be you.

Dan Kennedy said : "People are walking around with their umbilical cords hanging out, looking for a place to plug them in." Too true.

People will pay attention to you not just because you're going to give them great content (more on that later) but because you are interesting, and spookily EXACTLY WHO THEY WERE LOOKING FOR.

They will relate even more to you if your character has an interesting story to tell.

Think about this for a moment — name three things you learned at school.

Now name three of the characters from Seinfield. Or from Star Wars. Or from Friends.

People remember characters and relate to them. Stories keep people eagerly waiting for your next instalment.

Your mission then, is to create and use a character that will instil a sense of relationship with your posse (followers). You want them to feel like they know you already, as if you're their long-lost friend.

A good character is someone who is immediately recognisable. They stand for something, represent a belief, and has a back story (a legend) that sparks a sense of familiarity.

And a great character has magic powers. I put a lot of work into making sure my posse knows about, sees and is in awe of magic powers. Because of these powers I possess people pay attention to me.

For example, we offer the Mastermind Program to students of our Coaching Institute programs when they come along to our NLP Practitioner Training. I open this training with a demonstration of my magic powers. I find the person in the room (of 60 plus people) who has the worst phobia. I mean, they cry at the word of thing they're phobic about. They're convinced it can't be "cured", and they've been stuck with it for years. Often decades.

I then proceed, if they want me to, to help them get rid of the phobia. But I go further than that. As I'm "zapping" the participant with my magic powers I'm chatting about it to the room, like I'm just chatting to a friend, you know, all casual, making it all easy, inevitable, and "what's the big deal" kind of attitude.

Then as the phobia starts to disappear, I give it back to them.

And I just keep chatting.

Whole thing takes about twenty minutes, and if you took out the chat, it would be all over in five minutes. Then I teach the participant to get the phobia, and how to get rid of it, so they have the choice.

Then, if it's an elevator or height phobia, I send them off with a couple of people to take it for a spin, whilst I chat casually to the room, who are all, by now, sitting there with their jaws open, wondering what happened, and thinking "that looked about as easy as strolling out for a coffee."

How cool is that?

By the way, the really cool thing is I sell Mastermind on day five. What the heck does a phobia bust have to do with business building?

Nothing.

I don't care. I have demonstrated my magic powers, they will follow me, I am a character worthy of their attention and curiosity, even if it's just to see what the hell I'm going to do next.

I generate around $300,000 in sales in 1 hour on day five. Sometimes more. Never less.

Your magic powers are your unique abilities. In this niche, my magic powers are my ability to make millions of dollars in my own business, and to help others do the same.

And people want my magic power for themselves.

If you don't have your own magic powers you can borrow them from someone else until you have your own. You obviously wouldn't claim them as your own. You do this by focusing on the results others have achieved with the same XXX. You would acknowledge the source and as a result the prospect would make the implicit link between you and the other product.

Using metaphors

You need a story, or your message is too logical and boring. Stories create commonality and connection. They bring with them a great sense of familiarity and calm.

A persuasive metaphor allows a direct comparison between two unrelated things that transfers the favourable result and generates the desire to comply.

"Favourable result" means the desired outcome your posse wants.

"Desire to comply" means they will do what you want them to do, which is buy your stuff. Right?

So we talk about something seemingly innocuous, which ends up making your prospect want to give you money. It works because it's under the radar, and the prospect gets to think it's their idea to act.

Let's say we're going to sell a Mastermind ticket. That's $20,000 a ticket. I think the posse's fears are – "What if it doesn't work for me?" And "What if I'm not up to it?" For example, they're afraid of looking foolish, being the exception it doesn't work for, and having to learn something new.

All valid.

This business of running a business reminds me of when I went on my first horse riding trek. I had always wanted the feeling of being self sufficient, and I figured this would be the chance to give it a go.

But I didn't know the first thing about a horse riding trek, plus I didn't want to have to buy a whole bunch of stuff. Plus, my friends and family really thought I had lost my beans.

Anyway, I took the plunge and bought a trekking package. It was much easier than I thought it would be, and it only took me about two weeks to get everything set so I was ready to go. Plus, all I needed was the horse, which they gave me, and the equipment, which I rented from them.

The first day was a real sense of achievement. Not just for having a go, which was great, but because I was out in the wilderness, reliant on myself and the people I was with, who were experts, and learning how to do something I had never thought I'd be able to do.

Before I knew it, I was one week in and flying. The sense of freedom was something I cannot even find the words for. The feeling of achievement was unbelievable.

What's great now is I can always draw on that sense of achievement whenever I want to. It's made me know what I'm capable of.

Now I have an endless confidence, all from that first two weeks of planning and one week of doing the trek.

I guess the only downside is my friends and family who thought I was crackers want to do it too.

It was fun. More fun than I had anticipated.

If you go through this copy, you'll see I've dealt with the objections throughout, and built in what I know holds most people back – what if I don't love the experience because I'm not good enough?

I've pushed the message about self reliance and freedom, which is what it's all about.

I use phrases like "I took the plunge". That's me saying "I did it."

I also make it clear that it didn't need a lot from me, other than me committing. The experts supplied everything I needed.

Results were fast, too.

I have an endless source of good feelings about me.

I got a great result.

I had guidance from experts.

And now everyone else wants a piece of the action, so I wasn't as foolish as I thought I was, after all.

Main story lines

There are, according to Frank Kern, Jeff Walker and Dan Kennedy, three main storylines:

1. The reluctant hero.
2. The hometown person does good.
3. The "us-versus-them" storyline.

I always combine these story lines when marketing and selling. I never just rely on one. When combined you take your prospect through a range of emotions and thought patterns that will cause them to identify with and bond with you.

The reluctant hero allows you to sell something only because people are demanding it. What are you to do? You can't let all these people down. You'd rather be at home reading and studying, of course, because you're just a regular person and you're not that comfortable in the spotlight, and you've just stumbled upon this. The truth is, you have flaws just like everyone and you're just sharing all this magic as a favour to the posse.

It's like you're saying...

"I figured out some stuff, and it worked! I showed it to some other people, who thought it was cool, and you know what, it worked for them too. How great is that. It made us all money. I'm not usually teaching this stuff, I usually teach NLP and coaching, so if you can forgive my style, it's because this is not where I'm usually at. And please don't go and tell a bunch of people about it, because I've only got 150 tickets and that's it, because I want my quiet life."

The hometown boy does good storyline is thematically similar to the reluctant hero. It's like this...

"I was a regular coach, too. Just like you, and I was working so hard. I was working hard just to keep up with the demand, which is great, but you know what, it's insane, because I had no life. And I was getting tired. And I had no life. And I couldn't see any end in sight. It was just ridiculous, that my success was my failure. And it occurred to me that I had to change it, or I was never going to get out of the loop. I'd be trapped there forever. Never having a break unless I wanted to stop my income.

So I figured it out. I had to find a way to have people come to me, and I needed a system for that. So I spent $350,000 learning everything I could. Everything there was to be had. And I started using this stuff in my business, and you know what? It worked! So cool. And so much easier getting me out of that job and into a business where the profit wasn't because I was sitting with someone. Beautiful! Is that something like what you're looking for? Okay, let's talk."

Us-versus-them taps into the need to find someone else to blame for our troubles. It's – I was broke, or overweight, or shy or whatever. I had it all and I lost it. Then I found out...

And what I found turned my life around. And you know what? I'm going to share it with you.

And I turned it around despite the odds. And think if I can do it, you can.

Something like this...

> "I invested $350,000 in every program I could find. I have done them all from Frank Kern to Dan Kennedy. I've studied Tony Robbins, Michael Gerber, Brad Sugars, Mal Emery, Eben Pagan, Daryl and Andrew Grant.
>
> And they've all been worth the investment. All of them. I've earned my $350,000 back over and over and over. Which is great. But have you noticed something? You do all these courses and none of them actually give you all the steps in one place? There's a little bit of selling from the stage here, and over there's marketing. And here's a bit of how to have an ascension model. Here's how to sell a $25,000 program.
>
> No one puts it under one roof. It's not your fault you're wondering what to do next, no one tells you the exact steps. That's what Mastermind does..."

If you've seen me present, the above stuff is familiar to you!

Self esteem

Everyone has low self esteem about something, and some would argue that everyone has low self esteem on some level about themselves. No one has got it made, and no one has rock solid self esteem.

There is always a crack of doubt.

You don't want to prey on that. You want to take it into account.

I do more business when I talk smaller numbers than when I talk the giant numbers we actually do.

For example, you could say "Learn how to make $5,000 a day using this system" and leave it at that. A bunch of people would think "cool!" and a bunch more people would think, perhaps not even consciously "I could never do that."

How about this instead: "I did $5,000 a day, but you might not. But if you could do a fraction of that, how would that be?"

Matching your offer to your niche's desires

You have your niche, you have the desire, and now... what?

You need to come up with an offer that is going to match what your market wants, and you're going to need to develop the copy that conveys this match, so they opt in to your website so you can get their contact details so you can build a relationship with them.

Yup, it's a lot.

We're going to cover this in more detail in the next sections, but I want to explore with you here what's going to be happening, so you can see how important this step is.

After niche, this is the most important thing you will do. Ever. In marketing.

You could have identified a starving crowd, but unless you offer them the exact 'bait' for their details, they won't opt in. If they don't opt in, they're just spending your adwords budget and leaving.

This, more than anything, is where I put the most of my time and spend the most money and hire the best experts. You get the idea.

I don't ever throw something up onto the site and 'hope' it works. I will change the offer and how the lead finds it unless it is performing at a successful level.

A successful level is different for everyone. If we have 50 leads plus a week, we have a multimillion dollar business. If we have over 100 leads, we can't keep up with demand. If we have less than 50 leads, I fix it. Fast.

Let's look at:

www.ourinternetsecrets.com

as an example. This site is the work of my friends Andrew and Daryl Grant.

They've spent ages on getting the offer developed, based on everything they learned about their avatar.

Clearly not the same avatar as we have for Mastermind program. Yup, every niche has a different avatar. In fact, within The Coaching Institute, we have three different avatars. Certificate IV in Life Coaching, Diploma, and Masterminders.

All have different content, characters and stories sent their way. Anyway, back to the point of this.

But let's look at it – the offer, I think, is a pretty good match for what their avatar sees as their biggest problem. How do they make money online?

It's worth studying both our main sites and comparing the copy to the different markets, as a starting point to learning this. The sites are:

> www.thecoachinginstitute.com.au
> www.smallbusinessmastermindclub.com.au

10

The essential psychology of successful marketing

Our best evidence of what people truly feel and believe comes less from their words than from their deeds.

ROBERT CIALDINI

Marketing is the backbone of any business. You can have the best product in the world at the keenest price and available – but if nobody knows about it, you might as well have nothing.

People can't buy what they don't know about.

Marketing, as a concept, is very simple. You find out what people want. You give them what they want. You give them more of that and ask them to tell their friends.

Get any of the elements wrong, and business becomes difficult. Get them all wrong, and you go out of business. Get them right and make a fortune.

How marketing is done has changed over the years. Before television people used long sales letters to sell their stuff. And it worked. TV meant short spots for small fortunes had to be hired, so the long sales letter disappeared and 30 second spots replaced them.

Then the internet came along and long sales letters came back with a vengeance. You've seen them. And probably said you'd never buy anything from one of those things! You don't have to. Millions of people are, though. And billions is being made.

The great thing about the Internet is that the playing field is level again.

Anyone can go into business, market their stuff and make a fortune, without needing the TV advertising budget. I know dozens of home business owners who are making six figure incomes purely through running small internet businesses.

New technology may have opened up new marketing and distribution channels to us, but the rules of marketing – and business in general – remain the same. You still need to find a market; you still need to identify what they want; and you still need to work out how to communicate effectively with them so they buy from you. That hasn't changed.

What has changed is *how* we go about communicating with our target markets. The approach we can take to attracting the attention of our target market never been easier.

So to begin with, let's consider some of the laws that govern marketing in today's marketplace.

The Laws of Marketing

I think marketing comes down to one thing. Influence. Either you influence someone to buy your stuff, or they buy it from somewhere else.

It's the ability to shape another's choices.

Influence, then, is something that is very powerful and to needs to be understood – because, whether you intend to or not, you are, simply by being there, influencing your client. Quantum physics teaches us that we cannot observe something without that observation changing that which we observe. In other words, you can't *not* influence.

The question then becomes: do you do it well, or poorly? Do you do it so it's effective and produces great results for those around you, or is it hit and miss, with some results that you would, kindly, call inconsistent?

You are going to influence your followers/audience/clients whether you like it or not. Given this, it makes sense to influence effectively, with volition and with an understanding of basic rules of influence that, in marketing, make the difference between getting by and getting rich.

According to Dr Robert Cialdini, a retired professor of marketing, all influence is divided into six laws. We use all of these laws in our marketing, all the time.

Law 1: The Law of Reciprocity

Simply put, when you do a favour for someone, they believe they are indebted to you – they owe you, and will reciprocate when they can. If, for example, you give someone an unasked-for can of soda, they will accept it – then later, if you were to ask them to make a donation, they probably would.

This rule is paramount in our society; so much so that if we receive a small gift which we haven't asked for, we feel indebted to such an extent we will often do something far bigger in exchange.

The other way this works is this: if someone makes a large request, which is refused, they can then make a smaller request and have a much greater chance of acceptance. This is called the rejection-then-retreat technique.

Within this we can include the 'perceptual contrast' rule: if you buy an expensive suit, you are more likely to buy the jumper and shirts if you are offered them after the purchase (of the suit) than if you were offered it beforehand. After being exposed to the large-priced item, the smaller-priced ones seem even smaller in comparison. Combine the rules and its very powerful.

So how can you use this?

1. You give a sample of what you offer for free; and then you do it again, and again, and again. Then you ask for the business.

2. You offer a very expensive program first, then a smaller, more financially viable package second. It will be accepted more readily than if you had not made the expensive offer first.

Law 2: The Law of Commitment and Consistency

We will do a *lot* to appear consistent in our choices. Place a bet on a horse, and our belief it will win goes *up* after placing the bet, even though nothing has changed. We will do almost anything to justify our decision.

We convince ourselves we've made a great choice once a decision is made.

Automatic consistency – where we make up our minds so we can stop thinking about something – is also a high motivator. Once our minds are made up, the whole thinking about the issue fades because, after all, there are so many other things to think about.

Commitment is even more powerful – if I can get you to take a stand on something, I will have already set the stage for your possibly ill-considered consistency with the earlier commitment. Once the stand is taken there is going to be a desire within you to behave in ways that are stubbornly consistent to that stand. If you want, for example, to get the numbers of people who collect door-to-door to go up, you would call them earlier and run a survey in which you ask them how they would respond to being asked to door-knock for three hours. Many people, not wanting to seem uncharitable, will say of course! This, then, gets a whooping 700% increase in the numbers of people who will agree to actually collect for the charity.

What about this for the law of consistency and commitment: ask someone how they are and 33% will make the purchase. Say, "I trust you're well this evening," and it plummets to 15%.

It seems that if we state we are well and have committed to that answer, we have less excuses to say no to a simple request.

If someone is perceived a certain way, they will act consistently with that label if they think it is favourable to them.

You want testimonials from existing clients – it's an opportunity for them to be reminded of how good a decision they made.

If there are requirements for entry, it's perceived as more worthwhile and valuable. This is why there is hazing (rituals involving harassment, abuse or humiliation) in university boarding colleges in the US – so, how can you use this?

1. Get the paperwork, without the money, when someone is 'thinking about it'. If you don't get the paperwork, they will justify not signing. If you get the paperwork they will justify signing.

2. Either way, they will act on what they tell themselves and become convinced of.

3. With automatic consistency, you create it. What do you want your audience to accept without question, and stop questioning and thinking about? For example, how about you establish up front what their problem is – then reveal you have a five-step solution that is perfect for the problem (you've just told them they have) and they can only get the solution with you. This, by the way, pretty well sums up what online marketing is.

4. How about instead of saying "I trust you're well, this evening," say, "How are you this evening?" and wait for the answer. People committing to feeling great find it harder to say no.

5. Make the small sale, at the low level of the sales funnel, because it's the beginning of your client needing to feel consistent about their decision. They will come back, unless what they buy is no good, because they want to prove to themselves that they made the 'right' decision.

6. Tell someone they seem like someone who "likes to make things happen" and get their agreement on it ... now to appear consistent to this label, they will need to ... make things happen.

7. Get testimonials; lots of them – not just because new clients get to see how great you are, but because it takes care of your existing clients' need for consistency.

8. For your most elite membership, have requirements. Don't make entry such that they can afford it – make it more arduous. They will then perceive their membership as even more valuable.

Law 3: The Law of Social Proof

One of the means we use to find out what we think about something is to find out what everyone else thinks of it. Usually, when a bunch of other people does something, then it will be all right for us, too.

Most people, according to surveys, do not enjoy canned laughter. Yet, we still hear it. The reason is simple – we are more likely to laugh, and for longer, when it's there. Unfortunately, it's reflexive laughter, which means we didn't have to think for ourselves – but, again, it's making the amount of thinking we need to do less.

Have you ever noticed those jars on the counter near the cash register at restaurants? Tips are places in the jar before any are actually received just to get the ball rolling, and it works.

The same principle is used during telethons. You see, telethons tell us who's donating how much, just so we're reminded that everyone else is doing it. It's all a matter of numbers, isn't it? And it seems to be the more people the better – even to get rid of phobias – just have the child who's afraid of dogs watch videos of other children playing with dogs for 20 minutes a day and, within a month, the child can play with a dog and be fine. If it's one child they watch, it takes longer and is less effective.

Apparently, there is 'safety in numbers'.

Cialdini uses a different and lesser-known example to the one I use. In the Towers on 9/11, people were told by security to stay calm and not leave the second tower. Many listened and stayed at their desks. It seems that in the face of uncertainty, we don't want to appear flustered or not in control. We look for clues as to how to behave from those around us, and forget that everyone else is doing exactly the same thing. So everyone looks calm outwardly. The security guy said it was fine – so they stayed.

Cialdini talks about one of those events that intrigues and saddens me: the People's Temple of Jim Jones. Folk, who were largely uneducated and poor, gave up their freedoms of thought and action for the safety of the place where all decisions were made for them. The question asked by Cialdini is this: would they have still killed themselves had they remained in San Francisco? The answer is no. It was the alienation from the rest of the world, in a jungle and in a hostile country, that shaped their thinking and their actions. Cialdini doesn't mention the 24-hour-a-day broadcasting of Jim Jones over speakers throughout the compound. He does talk about how each member would have looked to the others for guidance when he gave the command to die. Eager action by highly compliant members would have provided clues as to how to respond; the gun-holding men around the edges of the compound would have discouraged rebellion. So, uncertainty with social proof is very powerful and dangerous; in this example, 900 people took their lives.

Law 4: The Law of Liking

We much prefer to say yes to requests from someone we know and like than anyone else. No surprise there. Tupperware parties are where this is used to its best. Various weapons of influence are present: reciprocity, commitment, social proof – and they all help things along. The true request for the purchase comes from the host – who is friends with everyone there.

The mention of a friend's name is enough.

We assign traits of talent, kindness, honesty and intelligence to good-looking people. It's called the 'halo effect' – one positive attribute dominates the way others view that person.

We like people similar to us. When the researcher dressed similarly to the subjects, he could borrow a dime two-thirds of the time. When he didn't, he managed less than half the time.

The number one salesperson in the world sent 13,000 cards out, every month, to all his clients. He was working on the principle that we believe praise about us, and believe people when they appear to like us.

We like things that are familiar to us. When shown a photo of yourself, you like it better if it's reversed, because that's how you are used to seeing yourself. Others, however, will prefer the photo of you not in reverse, for the same reason.

The principle of association governs both positive and negative connections – when we see something connected to something else we make associations. We see a beautiful girl next to a car and we believe the car goes faster and is better. Here's another example: we believe because it's the 'official' hair spray of the Olympics; it's somehow superior.

Now here's one that may surprise you. When we eat, we feel more positive about who we are with. Have you ever noticed that? I'm sure when you stop and think about it, you will nod in agreement. Amazing, isn't it?

So how can you use this?

1. Ask if the person you're dealing with heard about you from a client or a friend of yours.

2. If you can, and it's true, call someone and say, "X suggested I call you."

3. Make sure your photo on your website and brochures is professional and shows you at your best. Ensure your photo appears in plenty of places so the prospects are used to you.

4. Dress similarly when meeting with your prospects.

5. Write cards to prospects, and make it personal. Make it relevant to them, even if it's just to say 'happy holidays'.

6. Have positive images embedded in and around the text on your website and brochures.

Law 5: The Law of Authority

A researcher confronted participants in his experiment and told them that they had to administer electronic shocks to subjects who failed to 'remember'– and two-thirds of these participants administered every 'shock'. There was no real shock; the subjects were actors. However, one of the forty participants stopped when a subject 'begged' to end the experiment. The real culprit in this was not anything but a deep sense of duty to carry out the wishes of the researcher: a doctor in a white lab coat. (When they reversed the test and had the subject say 'continue' and the researcher say 'stop', 100% of the participants stopped immediately.)

We perceive greater authority, height, knowledge and credibility for titles, especially that of professor.

Clothes trigger responses too. Guard uniforms get a response far greater than regular clothes. Three-and-a-half times more pedestrians follow a jay walker in a suit than in regular clothes.

So how can you use this?

Dress for success. Joel Bauer talks about this *all* the time. Suits, dark; shirts, white. You can use some variance, but that's it. Shiny shoes, not scuffed. Neat nails. Neat hair, not too long. He says these can double your sales from the stage.

Law 6: The Law of Scarcity

The idea of potential loss plays a large role in our decision-making. We are more motivated by the thought of losing something than by the thought of gaining something of equal value. For example, more people want to insulate their homes when told how much money they could lose by inadequate insulation than if told how much they could save.

If it is rare, it is more valuable. This is why limited offers work. We decide quality based on availability – if it's too readily available, it must be less valuable.

We have a weakness for shortcuts.

We want what has been banned. This includes porn, guns, and tobacco. Keep an eye out for websites that say, 'they didn't want you to see this', or 'what the experts never wanted released', and you'll see what I mean.

Even scarcity of information boosts sales – tell someone your usual sales pitch and you'll sell. Tell them the pitch with a comment like, 'I'm going to run out of stock soon', and sales double. Then add, "And this information is not readily available to everyone. I only pass it on to you as you're my client …" – and sales boom again.

We like things more if we perceive them as being scarce.

So how can you use this?

1. Always have limited places for what you offer, especially as the price goes up.

2. Have a reason for this or you will be greeted with suspicion. As a coach, the spaces are limited because your time is limited.

The Bonus Laws of Influence

In Dan Ariely's book *Predictably Irrational*, we are introduced to a sensational law that is not used enough. I have taken what he says to heart and seen the results for myself. I have found the 'law of free' (as well as some other lesser known laws) to be so powerful, they doubled my business in 2009. And it was already doing millions in sales then.

Very early in Ariey's book he hits us with something that logic can't explain:

- Internet-only subscription for $59 – 16 students
- Print-only subscription for $125 – zero students
- Print and Internet subscription for $125 – 84 students

The majority of subscribers saw the advantage of the print and internet subscription. This makes sense. So what happens when he removes the 'decoy'?

Surely just as many people would subscribe to the third option? They should react the same way. This is what happened:

- Internet-only subscription for $59 – 68 students
- Print and Internet subscription for $125 – 32 students

What changed their minds? The presence or absence of the decoy is what influenced them. This is explained by what is called 'the law of relativity'.

According to this law, the third option is *enhanced* in value by the decoy.

The next study was with chocolates. The price of the Lindt was set at 15¢ and a Kiss at 1¢ – 73% bought the Lindt and 27% bought the Kiss. Pretty rational as they shopped on the quality of chocolate – the Lindt was a truffle. Then they reduced the price of the Lindt to 14¢ and the Kiss to zero. All they had done in effect was to lower both prices by just 1¢. So what happened? Remarkably, 69% went for the free chocolate while sales of the Lindt fell from 73% to 31%.

Most purchases have an upside and a downside built into them. When you make something free, we forget the downside of the purchase.

FREE! gives us such an emotional charge that we perceive what is being offered as immensely more valuable than it really is. We are afraid of loss. Remember, we do more to avoid pain than we do to feel pleasure. There is no perceived possibility of loss when it's free. Therefore, in the land of pricing, FREE! is not just another price!

This brings us neatly to 'the law of free'. This is where the message 'FREE!' blinds us to logic.

Now that you have a better understanding of some of the lesser-known laws that govern how we perceive things when we make purchasing decisions, it's time to turn our minds to ways we can put this to good (or effective) use in our businesses.

11

Making business easy to do: Understanding value-based marketing

Most small business advertising and marketing stinks. Monstrous sums are wasted, and opportunities lost.

DAN KENNEDY

When marketing is done right, it makes selling easy, predictable and profitable. Value-based marketing will, when done right, sift, sort and screen people who you want to talk to and do business with. It is the quickest way to the sale.

Most traditional business owners run their marketing campaigns in what I call a haphazard trial-and-error fashion, jumping from one idea to the next while listening to what newspaper and magazine sales reps feed them. When I think of this, I can't help seeing an image in my mind of them throwing mud at a wall and hoping some of it will stick.

For you to fully understand the power of a systematic, structured value-based marketing campaign, you need to understand that everything we do is systematically aimed at finding clients who are pre-interested, pre-motivated, pre-qualified and pre-disposed to doing business with us.

A system built on these fundamental principles will, if properly implemented, bring a hungry posse of prospects automatically to your door.

This is why it is critical for you to know that what I am working towards here is building you a diversified group of systems that automatically delivers ideal prospects, predictably and dependably, and in the right quantity. This is the real difference between traditional (or manual) marketing and real (value-based) marketing.

What value-based marketing is not

One lesson I have leant over the years is that knowing what not to do is as important as knowing what to do. This was an important lesson because, when it comes to value-based marketing, the one thing it is not doing is getting your name out there. It isn't about name recognition. It isn't about building an image. It isn't about getting your name in front of as many people as you can. It isn't about bragging about how excellent you are.

Value-based marketing is not about copying the Fortune 100 companies' inane or funny advertising strategies. Neither is it cold prospecting. It's not begging people for referrals. It's not about attending network meetings and social events to meet clients or prospects. It's not manipulation or unethical tactics. It isn't taking people to lunch or playing golf. It is not having a fancy brochure and business card. It's not having a website or being very good at what you do. It's not winning an award, having letters after your name, or a plethora of business achievement certificates on your wall.

Marketing these days is a very sophisticated 'art'. Some go so far as to call it a science. I call it sophisticated, because we do know how it works: what to do to get better results, how to test and measure our efforts, and how to fine tune a message so that it consistently produces the results we want.

This applies even more to value-based marketing.

But due to its very nature, for value-based marketing to be truly effective, it needs to be built on a solid and reliable platform. And it is this that I will be concentrating on next. Of course, what I am about to discuss can't be exhaustive, because the subject is so dynamic and exciting that it is constantly changing, even though some of the basic fundamentals will underpin much of it.

The educational spectrum

Any business can gauge its success, not from how many widgets it makes, but from how many it sells. Making widgets is the lowest level of skill. The highest level of skill is turning a widget into a solution that people must have to solve their problems – again, and again, and again.

As a business owner, you probably know how to make the widgets, and how to make them well. The trick is understanding the process a prospective buyer goes through before making the decision to buy – from you. Once you have a general idea of this, marketing becomes so much easier. By that, I mean it makes so much more sense to structure it in certain ways that are designed to bring results – time and time again.

So what is the process someone goes through before making the decision to buy? According to *Monopolize Your Marketplace:*

http://www.y2agency.com/monopolize.html

there are generally nine steps to this:

1. The prospect first gets the idea to buy what you sell (or they switch vendors).

2. They start gathering information on an informal basis. They ask friends and associates for recommendations.

3. They commence heavy-duty fact-finding.

4. They narrow choices through a process of elimination They begin narrowing in on favourites; a decision is coming soon.

5. They make the decision to buy, but not necessarily who to buy from.

6. They wait for the timing to be just right.

7. Money changes hands.

Most marketing pieces only appeal to *now* buyers. Problem is, those who are ready to buy now only account for between one and five percent of all prospects. By putting a low-risk offer in your ad that allows the prospect to get more information – to become more educated – you can capture a much larger portion of prospective buyers.

Human nature demands that buyers always want to make the best decision possible. Marketing and advertising should get the attention of the target market, facilitate their decision-making processes, and lower the risk of taking the next step in the selling process.

Being the trusted advisor

Your job, then, is not to jump on every lead that comes along and try to close them unless... UNLESS they trust you.

Value-based marketing is about building a relationship with your prospect, through samples of what you can do for them, case studies of what has worked for others like them, email campaigns that build the relationship through providing value to the prospect.

And you don't talk about yourself.

You talk about them. Their challenges. Their desires. Their goals and ambitions. You share how to achieve those goals, by giving samples of your stuff to them for free.

You let them, as they move through the educational spectrum, come to see you as a trusted advisor.

Designing your marketing campaign using value-based marketing

Use this checklist to ensure you've covered every aspect of value-based marketing (much of this is covered in detail throughout this book):

- Find a niche (an inch wide and mile deep)
- Get clear on your avatar
- Match your message to the market by being the character they would find attractive and desirable

- Develop something about you and your business that is unique
- Focus on what's in it for your clients; it's not about you
- Use a lead generation marketing system
- Always capture your clients' details – especially their email addresses
- Have a compelling offer
- Use a sequential marketing system – at least 3 steps
- Use testimonials and social proof in all your marketing
- Use Cialdini's laws of influence when marketing
- Use big benefit headlines
- Add massive value that far exceeds what the client dreamed would be available
- Add irresistible bonuses that make buying your stuff worth doing just to get the bonuses
- Use a big bold guarantee that eliminates the risk for the client
- Have a call to action – tell the prospect or client what to do next
- Always account for the lifetime value of the client
- Focus on back end sales as much as front end sales
- Track all your marketing carefully

12

Why the internet is the best way to make money while you sleep

The internet is the cheapest place to fail.

BRETT MCFALL

What is online marketing

Online marketing is what you do through a website or emails. It compares to offline marketing, which is mailouts, faxes and postcards.

I love online marketing simply because there are potential clients out there right now who can't find you and don't even know you exist. And with the Internet, they can find me.

Picture this: you're networking and you know the person you're chatting with won't really be into buying whatever you're offering right now – but they would love a free report because it might just help them out. You recommend the report to them; you say it's free, and you let them know where they can get it. A day later, you notice the same person has opted in, given their details and is now quite happy to stay in touch with you through your regular email contact, free gifts – and even may respond to an offer to spend money when the time is right.

Or, you're networking, you ONLY offer the opportunity to buy your widget – and the person you're chatting with is not in the mood nor has the time for it. You part ways, never to meet again. No business done. Next.

I'd rather have someone's contact details as well as their permission to market to them than to try to convince them to buy from me right now. I'd rather create followers who become clients when they're ready than push it because I need a client.

Why do we need to get good at this? Or at least not suck at it! Here are my reasons:

Reason One (otherwise known as the rubbish website)

I've done the research and it frightened me. People generally stay on a website for seven seconds, unless something captures their interest. Seven seconds – that's nothing!

So it brought home to me, in sharp focus, how important it was to have a website that was going to GRAB people and make them want to stay, and then PLAY.

Reason Two (otherwise known as 'the problem of the tourist')

How many times have you been to a strange town, wondered around, seen some cool shops and never been able to find your way back there again? Who am I kidding? I still do this in Melbourne, and I've been here for 16 years!

Well, this is what happens to your prospects every day – they arrive on your website, stay about seven seconds, leave in a rush thinking that was cool, and then have no idea where they were so never come back.

By the way, less than 4% of people will ever return to the average website. Shudder!

If they won't come to you, then you have got to have a way of going to them.

Reason Three (otherwise known as 'you think you're an expert')

The best way to get clients (and a following) is to be the expert in your field. One of the best ways to achieve this is to have a strong presence in the mind of your prospect.

So you need to reach them. And if you're advertising, you're reaching them more than once in that rare blue moon that they stumble across your ad more than once. And given that conventional marketing wisdom says you need seven touches to make a sale, what else are you doing? Emails. Free stuff. Newsletter with more free stuff. Interview – free (but you knew that). Give them resources that they didn't expect. All online. All automated. All reminding them that you seem to be turning up everywhere.

You want them to think, "Man, this gal/guy MUST be good!"

Reason Four (otherwise known as 'some people just work too hard')

So, you want to have a holiday, and you're wondering how you're going to do it when, in reality, it means your income is simply going to stop. It's driving you a little nuts, what with the long hours you're putting in without being able to take a much-needed break. And then you realise that if you have an effective online presence, your marketing will be hard at it 24/7 all year round, regardless of what you're doing in real time.

Cool, you say.

Reason Five (otherwise known as 'there is your local economy and there is your world economy')

It's a big world. There are clients in your local area and there are clients who you will find at your nearest and dearest networking event who will work with you.

But there is a planet full of potential clients you won't ever meet unless you get online.

Online marketers have known for years what the rest of us are just starting to realise – people DO buy online. They like the convenience and the security of being able to stay in their own home and still get cool stuff delivered right to their door.

Reason Six (otherwise known as 'it's cheaper than rent')

You can rent offices and go to the expense of setting up a good-looking office with all the expected bells and whistles – or you can take $500 and get started. You're only ever $500 away from bailing if the idea is a dud. This option certainly has a low downside.

Reason Seven (otherwise known as 'your business IS your database')

Your business value does not lie in that cool widget that you're proud of. Even the most fabulous widget in the world is a dud unless it has... buyers and potential buyers.

The real value is in your database.

The bigger the database, the more the value goes up – but only as long as the database is made up of people who are interested in (and preferably passionate about) the subject that you are niched in.

The tighter and more relevant the database, the more valuable your business is. I'm not saying this so you can plan to sell your business, although that would be a possibility. I'm saying it so you understand that you will make money if you have a database of relevant potential clients.

We don't have a huge database, but it's full of people who like what we do, are interested in the same things we are, who enjoy what they're learning from our newsletters, and who thank us for sending them reminders that we're here. Some of them have never spent a cent with us, but they still love staying in touch and like what we do. They talk to people, so the cycle stays active.

And sometimes, years after our relationship first got started, they join a program.

Reason Eight (otherwise known as 'it beats cold calling')

I am a cold calling legend! I am one of those freaks who loves it, and I am good at it. Most people aren't, I have to say – and that's just the way it is.

So how would you like it if you never had to do another cold call again? Or perhaps more accurately, how cool is it that you'll never have to go cold calling in the first place?

You don't have the power when you call them. You're in the backseat, and it's easy for them to say 'no', because who are you anyway?

But if they inquire with you, it's completely different. You're now in the driver's seat. They requested more information. They provided you with their contact details. They have expressed an interest in your thing. They have invited the interaction.

Yes, things may take a little longer as they get to know you, but it beats a week of people saying 'no' on the phone. AND, if you're cold calling, you only get to tell the people you reach about you, and only once at that. They don't get to then start building a relationship with you.

You want the time to build the relationship. You want them to know they can trust you. You see, the fact is: no trust, no sale.

So instead of reaching only five people when you call them, you reach hundreds of people who are actively searching for the exact solution you offer.

I could go on with many more reasons for marketing online, but here's the biggest one:

Reason Nine (otherwise known as 'how long has this been going on')

It's not unusual for me to make in excess of $250,000 to $500,000 a MONTH using the systems I'm teaching you. If you're now not completely convinced of how powerful this is as a marketing medium, I'm going back to Paris.

Understanding your online buyers

Marketing is all about understanding the needs of your prospects and then letting them know that you have a solution to their problem. And as I have mentioned before, to do this effectively, there are a number of smart things you could do to improve your chances of doing so profitably.

When it comes to understanding the needs of your prospects, the first thing you need to take into consideration is what's going on in their minds. By this I mean you need to have an understanding of their mindset when they are looking for a solution to one of their problems. This will give you some heavy clues as to how to catch their attention and appeal to them. You need to know how to make them sit up and take notice of your marketing pieces.

Once again, I'll be skipping over how this applies to traditional of-fline marketing here as this has been extensively covered in other publications. What I do want to focus on, however, is how this applies to online marketing.

When someone decides to look for a solution to a problem, they will tend to do so online in the first instance. It doesn't matter if they are thinking of upgrading their car or their home, or if they are looking for a cure for a headache – the first, easiest and most unthreatening place they will go to in the first instance is their computer.

Once there, they will generally look for information (which they hope will steer them in the right direction and, ultimately, to a decision) from websites, blogs and emails.

Let's take a closer look at each.

Websites

People look at websites with a problem/solution mindset. They are looking for information that has a direct bearing on their problem. For instance, they may be looking for a cure to a cold.

The mindset they are in can be described as 'ready to buy'. They are looking for deals and value.

Blogs

When people are looking for news about something, or to find out what the latest gadgets are, they do so with a 'news-getting' frame of mind. But bear in mind that they would not use a typical search engine here; they're not looking for everything concerning a particular topic: they are looking for only one or two. Blogs are great for this.

Email

People are usually in a different state of mind again when opening up their emails – I call it the 'let's be productive' or 'what's up with so-and-so' frame of mind.

If you take out the work part of it, you're left with interaction with friends. So when someone checks emails, we're left with relationship stuff; it's the main reason why people check their email.

They're almost never wondering if you've sent them an offer in an email. They want funny stuff, responses from friends and people they know, and then work stuff.

With this in mind, when sending a prospect an email, offer them CONTENT to get them – but to keep them, you must become a character.

We remember and respond more to entertainment than we do to useful content. So, on DAY 1 send lots of content and introduce yourself to the character – tell them who you are and why they can relate to you. Then, by DAY 7 you focus more the being the character; what you stand for, why you're great, why they should trust you, and less on content.

As time progresses, ease off on content and build up the character.

13

Generating highly targeted, high-value leads

The list is king.

JEFF WALKER

Jeff's right. The list is king. But you don't want any list of prospects on your database. You want a quality list. A quality list is responsive – they do what you ask them to do, and they will buy what you offer.

It's pointless having thousands of names on a list if none or very few of them buy anything from you.

To give you an example of this, I make about $1,000,000 per thousand names on our list.

19 ways to build your list

In this digital age, most people simply can't be without their computers. In fact, recent research suggests that if most people had to choose, they would rather go without eating than be offline for a day. Most progressive marketers know this and have structured their businesses in such a way that they have an impressive or compelling online presence.

They know the importance of communicating with their existing and prospective clients through the Internet. One of the ways they do this is through online subscriptions.

So, how do you go about increasing your subscription base? Experience shows that if you build a targeted group of hungry subscribers, you'll grow your online income. What you want is a *targeted* group of subscribers – not just a general list. You want a *hungry* group of subscribers.

They need to be targeted to your specific subject – and they need to be hungry for more information on the topic. In addition, you need to build a *relationship* with those subscribers.

Here's how to go about it:

Lead generator #1: Pay-Per-Click advertising:

This is, by far, my favourite way of generating targeted traffic. Google AdWords gives me exactly the type of lead I want for my businesses, because to find me they had to type in exactly the key words my services are a match for.

Before AdWords, we were relying on newspaper advertising, which was ridiculously expensive, hit a mass population who weren't my avatar, resulted in few calls and next to no business.

After AdWords we receive hundreds of leads every month.

Lead generator #2: Write articles to generate traffic and build back links:

With article marketing your goal is to write high-quality articles that are informative and useful for the readers. You want the article to establish you as the undisputed expert in your field. You want it to impress the reader enough that they click through to your website.

Lead generator #3: Focus your webpage on generating subscribers:

If you're on AdWords there's every chance someone is going to click through from your ad and check out your website.

What you don't want is a pretty site that tells them all about you. You want a site that gives them something really cool, in return for their contact details.

This means always listing your subscribe offer in a premium position on your website (top right).

Lead generator #4: Speak at events and invite people to visit your site and receive something you've created especially for them for free:

I like this one much better than networking and trying to find a buyer.

Instead of giving out your business card, how about collect lots of business cards and give the people a free report?

Lead generator #5: Have a blog:

If you don't have a blog, set one up TODAY. This is one of the best tools I've seen to help you generate free search engine rankings. Go after a competitive search term for your main blogging site.

Lead generator #6: Create blog posts that target long tail search terms:

The tool I highly recommend going through regularly is the Google Keyword Tool. If you're aggressively going for the subscriber and you start generating search engine visitors, you will grow your list.

Lead generator #7: Work on generating incoming links:

We have an arrangement with our clients that if they link to us, we will link to them. These reciprocal links mean hundreds of links for us, but only one link for them. The advantage for them is that because Google likes our site, the link to them is rewarded by Google with a higher ranking.

Remember, what Google actually does is a complete mystery to anyone. And they can change their minds at any time, and this idea goes the way of the dodo.

Lead generator #8: Link out to other good blogs in your niche:

You could put them in the blogroll. You might do linking posts where you link to other people's best content. Or you might link inside your article itself. Those bloggers will see your link and you'll likely get them to at least visit you (building potential partners in the market).

Lead generator #9: Set up a 'landing page':

Set up a landing page where the only thing that can occur on this page is for the potential subscriber to enter their contact details in return for receiving a cool free thing. When you set this page up, make sure it's built into the framework of your multi-page site – Google does not like single page contact-capture sites and have removed them from Google.

Check out:

www.smallbusinessmastermindclub.com.au/lead-generation

for an example of this. This is a landing page that only appears as a sponsored ad when people type in certain key words. When the potential subscriber clicks on the ad they are directed this landing page (sometimes called a squeeze page) and their main options are to enter in their contact details in return for free stuff they want.

The page itself is part of the main website:

www.smallbusinessmastermind.com.au

so that it's not a standalone single page site.

This way we can run various landing pages at different times, testing and measuring which ones work the best.

Lead generator #10: Contact list owners in your market about your excellent low-cost item:

Give them a free copy of your cool thing and set them up as an affiliate so they can promote it. Affiliates are one of the best ways to generate responsive subscribers.

Don't just do the normal product affiliate offers to potential JV partners. Offer to write them some exclusive content, do an interview with them, or link to them from your blog to begin building a relationship.

Lead generator #11: Create videos based on keyword phrases people are searching for:

Use the Google Keyword tool to see what people are searching for. Create a simple video teaching them the subject. Then add in a link to your site in the description and the video itself. Add the videos to YouTube and to Google Video.

Upload your video to multiple video sites at once (for free) using a site such as:

www.tubemogul.com

Lead generator #12: Create a FAQ (frequently asked questions) file for a popular forum in your market:

When someone asks one of those questions, post your FAQ response along with your resource box (which is a link to your subscribe page).

Lead generator #13: Give away one of your paid products to another marketer in your field:

Let them give it away to any of their buyers. Of course, make sure this has a call to action for them to buy one of your items or to get on your list. You make nothing from this sale, but you're being put in front of their buyers.

Lead generator #14: Sell reprint rights to some of your products:

You'd do this also to be exposed to a new group of buyers. You make money from selling the reprint rights licence, but you're also having other people generate leads and backend customers for you.

Lead generator #15: Do interviews and teleconferences:

One of the fastest ways to get a surge of new subscribers is through doing a teleconference or an interview with someone who has a list of their own. In exchange for your time, you'll likely generate sales and subscribers.

Lead generator #16: Create a joint product with other experts in your market:

This can be a low-cost lead item. Make sure to have your call to action for your freebie signup in this product. Even if you never sell a copy, the other experts will be generating backend subscribers and sales for you.

Lead generator #17: Ask an additional question instead of just for their email address and name:

Ask them for their biggest question or what they're looking for today. Most list building services do have the ability for a custom question which you can use to find out more about your subscribers.

Lead generator #18: Mail an invitation to get the free report to your ideal clients in your area:

Wait until they come to you. A week later follow up with a postcard to remind them (11 business owners have already received the report and are benefitting from it).

Lead generator #19: Be on Face book:

My friend Dale Beaumont does this better than anyone I know. He has a fan page, and people 'like' it, which gets all their friends checking it out. He has generated hundreds of leads doing this.

Getting someone to opt-in online

Your opt-in page is VITAL to your business success. Gone are the days when the standard website is good enough.

All the usual items on most web sites have one thing in common – they're about YOU. Understand that prospects aren't interested in you at this stage; they're interested in themselves and getting a solution to their problems. What stops them finding out if you can help them is that you've gone on about yourself and not how you can help them. It seems so simple when you get it, but it took me about five years before I realised how powerful this really was.

Traditionally, we're supposed to tell people about us so they can know how good we are. Isn't that why people buy?

Not a chance!

They need to build trust, and with your opt-in page you help them feel that trust – you also get to:

1. Help them get to know you.

2. See how you can help them.

3. Get them sampling your stuff so they can see if you're a good fit for them.

4. Become familiar to them so they feel they know you.

5. Let them know you're not going anywhere.

All of these benefits will help your prospects feel they can trust you enough to try you out. They might not go for the top-of-the-line product you sell, but they may go for a smaller purchase that lets them see what you have to offer.

The opt-in page

The opt-in page is the webpage you create so that prospects can leave their details in return for some free cool stuff.

Benefits over regular sites

The biggest benefit is that it stops people getting distracted and looking at other stuff that isn't going to help them make the decision to leave their details. All you're aiming to do is GET THEIR CONTACT DETAILS.

The other benefit is you get to give them exactly what you want; or, if you can't give them exactly what they want, they leave – which is good because they were never a match for your services anyway.

The third benefit is that you help the prospects because they only have to make one decision. Most sites offer stacks of things to do, to look at, to read and to make decisions about. Your opt-in page (landing page, squeeze page) is going to offer only one thing: to give them some free stuff in return for their details. That's it. Nothing else.

What does an opt-in page involve?

The opt in page has on it, (probably, but not absolutely):

1. A great headline
2. A short video (optional)
3. A few bullet points that are solution-based comments
4. A call to action (leave contact details in return for free stuff)

The headline

This can be the toughest part to get right. Your headline is going to be a question, a statement or a command that addresses the NUMBER ONE ISSUE your prospect has. It addresses nothing else. The best place to start to learn how to write a great headline is to check out some good ones online. To find some, type 'internet marketing' into your search engine and check out the opt-in pages you'll find in the sponsored sites.

Another way to know what to do for a headline is to check out some women's magazines. They have the best headlines, and they tell you what is topical!

The video

This is important – ONLY use the steps you're about to hear about; don't *ad lib* or add something just because you like it.

Check out:

http://www.dotcomsecrets.com

and you'll see it's not a simple opt-in page like we've talked about, but once you opt-in, watch as you get sent emails of offers – and you follow the link and you land on … an opt-in page.

Now, down the track, once you're up and flying, you can develop a site like this. I'd suggest EXACTLY like his, because it has the ascension model built right into it, and has thousands of followers who buy everything it suggests.

For now, as we begin our climb to online credibility, we start where this site did, with an opt-in page that doesn't confuse or distract from our message of wanting their contact details.

Check out:

http://www.andrewanddaryl.com/

for a simple opt-in page.

So you have the headline, and now your video content. Just include:

1. Your name.
2. Your business.
3. What you have.
4. Why they need it.
5. How they can get it (fill in their details).

That's it. They fill in their details, you get to send them free stuff.

14

Turning traffic into profit with email campaigns

Use what talents you possess; the woods would be very silent if no birds sang there except those that sang best.

HENRY VAN DYKE

It's one thing to get the lead, it's another to convert them into paying clients.

We're pretty good at this. In fact, many of the top marketers in Australia fly in to see how we do business, so they can replicate our results.

What do we do?

We make sure every single lead is treated like the solid gold it is.

This applies particularly to your online presence. The one important function your virtual presence has is to sell. Your website, your blogs and your emails are all doing a selling job for you while you are doing what you do best – running your business.

How to write good emails

There are some things that can make a huge difference to the success of your email marketing campaign. And remember, you need to regard each and every email you send as part of your sales arsenal.

Here are 16 tips that can really help increase the sales from an email marketing campaign. The key is to have your clients look forward to getting your emails, and to open and read them as soon as they arrive.

Also, clients should take whatever action you ask them to take – click on a link, download a file, sign up to a teleseminar, or whatever.

It is an art to write emails like this. Here are the 16 key things you can do that can help:

1. Provide what the prospect wants

We are constantly listening to our prospects, seeing what they are attracted to, and finetuning our message because of what we learn.

If you receive emails from people on your list asking you questions, this provides you really useful information about what people are after.

Another way is to ask prospects directly. Email out a short survey giving them a list of problems or issues (to which you have a solution), and ask them which ones are most important to them.

You can have a blog where people can post comments so you know what's on their minds.

Once you have a handle on this, you can design your emails around what most people are saying they most want.

2. Write a subject line that gets your emails opened

How many emails do you delete each day? How many emails do you delete without even looking at them?

One of the main reasons that email marketing will fail is because people don't even read it. You want to increase the odds of your email being opened and read by writing a good subject line.

The subject line of an email serves the same purpose as the headline of your sales letter – to get people to read it. So spend some time on it. Your subject line works best if it either creates curiosity or gives a benefit (or both). For example: This is what the survey showed ...

One subject headline that we use is: Bad news...

It works better than all the rest!

3. Have one clear purpose for your email

Decide up front the one purpose of your email, and ensure that the whole email points to this. Never try to accomplish more than one thing with an email.

If your purpose is to have the reader download a free report, then talk about the benefits of receiving it. Make them feel like they will miss out on something important if they don't download it.

Don't get caught up selling anything (which is the job of a later email when you invite them to a teleseminar).

We might have an email that invites people to request a report. They have to email us their request, and that way we know who is the most responsive.

4. Personalise your subject line and email content

Most autoresponder systems have the ability to add your client's name (and sometimes other details) to your email subject line and message.

This is not something you want to do all the time, but used occasionally, it can work well. Mixing it up (sometimes using names, sometimes not) makes your emails look more personal.

Whatever you do, you don't want it to look like they're one of thousands of other people. Everyone has a sign over their heads saying: Make me feel special.

5. Forget the hype

Nothing too over-the-top. Don't be dramatic, overly excited, or 'salesy'.

Statements like 'trust me, you'll kick yourself in a couple of hours if you miss this one' are going to turn people off. You need to be enthusiastic, but make sure you include the reasons why you are so excited.

How is what you have going to *really* help your reader? Give reasons, and be specific about them. Give examples, and proof. They're not interested in superlatives like 'amazing', 'fantastic', or 'unbelievable'. Your prospect is interested in the specifics of what the recommended product or service did for you or your clients.

In fact, the more specific the better. For example: Jacqui completed her first part of the training exactly 15 days ago and already has one paying client. She attributes her success to using the "Seven Steps to Your First Client" system she received at her training. If you would like to receive these steps, then email... etc.

6. Tailor your message to the avatar

One way to do this is to set up different lists according to what or if people have bought from you in the past. Let me give you an example of how this could work. Say for example, you have a list of non-buyers. To this list, first market your product using a series of emails. Once they have bought your product, transfer them to another list and market your next product, and so on.

We divide our lists depending on the different avatars we have.

7. Use an informal tone

Your clients are more likely to buy from you if they see you as a trusted friend and advisor. One way to do this is to use a conversational and informal tone in your emails.

Imagine you're writing it to a friend you know well, rather than to a group of people, some of whom you've never met. I know I've done a good job when people email me back as if they are the only one I've written to.

I write our marketing emails as if it's me writing to one person. I don't say "Hey everyone". I say: How are you?

8. Be the character your avatar is attracted to

When writing your emails, don't just be informal, be the character they are attracted to. Your job is to be interesting, so they keep opening the emails you send.

9. Provide great value

This is a great way to build trust and responsiveness, and to continue to build yourself as the trusted friend and advisor. Giving people tips, answering questions they may have or giving them links to useful resources is a great way to build the client relationship.

You want to get many emails each week thanking you for the information and support you provide in your emails. This can also help you to stand out from the bulk of marketing emails that contain calls to action but little in the way of value.

10. Make your emails look like they are written by a person, not a machine

Just because your autoresponder system can wrap lines so they're shorter and justify the right hand side, doesn't mean you should!

Avoid looking overly 'perfect'. Aim to make your email look as if it has been personally written by you, just for them.

You want to avoid looking too impersonal. And people don't like to be one of many.

11. Make your emails short

Emails are disposable. They are easy to delete. They are easy to forget.

If you send an essay, you'll be put in recycling after lunch.

Say only what needs to be said. Remember to be interesting – a character they are curious about.

12. Make your call to action clear

If you send an email, make sure what you want the prospect to do is very clear. Ideally, repeat the action you want them to take.

For example:

> ...for your copy of this report click here.
>
> Here's to your success,
> Sharon Pearson
>
> P.S. Here's where you get your copy of the report "Seven Minutes to Seven Figures"

13. Sometimes don't use autoresponders

We mix our autoresponders with emails we have created especially for that day. For example, if we have run a training, we might send an email to our prospects letting them have a 'peek' at part of the training we had recorded.

If there is an event coming up we might send an email letting people know there are still a couple of seats left, and include a bonus for the first two people who decide to come along.

14. Use an effective P.S.

I don't remember who told me this, but apparently many people jump straight to the end of the email and read the last line or so.

Whatever is your most important message goes into the P.S.

Whatever you want them to do goes into the P.S.

And you can have a P.P.S.

15. Test your emails before you send them our to your list

We send our marketing emails to ourselves first, to make sure they look okay, that nothing was lost in the process and that they present the way we intended. Lots of mistakes have been picked up that way.

16. Always measure and fine-tune

Your autoresponder program should be able to tell you what percentage of the emails you sent were actually opened by the recipient. As you test different subject lines or personalisation options, keep track of the stats. If it doesn't work, replace it.

15

Create massive profits in minimal time with product launches

Tens of millions of dollars have been made in product launches in every niche imaginable with every product imaginable.

JEFF WALKER

Developing the ideal product

If you get clear on your avatar and on the character you need to be for that avatar, then the next piece of the puzzle is to work out what content they want more than anything.

Product design is never: build it and they will come.

It's they come and what do they want when they get here?

You ask them – as we have already talked about, and you get very clear on what problems they want solved and what solutions they want delivered.

Only then can you think about putting together your product.

For example, our Certificate IV in Life Coaching avatar is Jacqui, who wants to believe in herself, feel great about what she does, and have the sea change without moving house. For her the Certificate IV in Life Coaching is perfect because it offers many hours of personal development, helps her get clear on who she is, what drives her, what her passions are and what her purpose is.

The program focuses on one-on-one coaching and opportunities for her to be around like minded people. It delivers support for life, for free with a class every fortnight, forever.

It's attractive to her, but not to our Diploma of Life Coaching avatar, who wants financial freedom through coaching and training, wants to develop an online presence and wants to run seminars and sell products.

Our Diploma avatar is more 'serious' about making it as a coach, gets the business realities of the more education you have in this area the better and they're willing to do much more work to get the much greater result.

Each program is designed very specifically for the different avatars and we put a lot of effort into making sure this is improved and adapted as we learn more about what they want.

You can develop products cheaply and easily in a wide range of formats:

- CD's
- DVD's
- Teleseminar series
- Training programs
- Mentoring
- Home study program
- Training delivered in Camtasia
- A series of classes
- A series of Mastermind groups

Or any combination of any of these.

The product launch

A product launch is a gradual series of events that build anticipation, intrigue and desire for your product or service.

If you simply announce your new product to the market place, you won't have created any buzz around it. However, if you slowly create anticipation, and only release the product when people really want to know about it, and just have to have it, not only can you potentially make millions of dollars in a short space of time, but your product can then endure for the long haul.

One of my mentors assisted in a product launch that did over $20 million US.

We have clients who regularly do product launches worth tens of thousands of dollars.

Credit for this formula goes to Jeff Walker and his Product Launch Formula program.

Firstly you need to set up a separate email list that is dedicated to the product launch. Then, send an email out to your entire list, letting them know that something exciting is coming soon. If you would like to receive updates on this and when it will be available, please let us know by registering your email on this page.

You do this so you don't overwhelm your full list with stuff they might not want. You only want people who have chosen to hear more about it. That way you don't 'burn' your list and have people opting out.

Don't discuss the product straight away. You want to build interest and desire through giving little snippets of the actual content. These samples should be your best stuff and have people buzzing about it.

You also want to ask them what their biggest frustration or challenge is. Then go ahead and solve it for them in a blog. You email the list, say thanks for the question, and for the answer, go here... and send them to the blog.

Some emails will suggest a promise of what is to come:

> Next week I'll share with you the Number One Way to
> XXX in 5 Days or Less... Look out for that email.

You mix up the delivery methods of the content. One piece of content may be in the form of a video. Another may be a class with you on the phone. Another may be an MP3 they can download. You can use PDF reports, templates and checklists. Ryan Diess, another Internet marketer into launches, recently gave away free software as part of his free samples leading up to his launch.

Then when you're ready to launch you can do one of a few things.

You can simply send an email saying:

> We've discussed a lot of challenges over the past few weeks, and I've provided a lot of solutions. But it's only part of the whole picture. Mark in your diary next <INSERT DATE AND TIME HERE> and because that's when I'm making a pretty big announcement about how to get my whole formula for How to XXX.

Then you send an "It's LIVE!" email with a link to the purchase page.

We do it a little differently. We sizzle, then on the launch day they send us an email saying they're in, and in return, once they've done the paperwork, they receive a free cool thing, like a computer.

We do this because our price points are high.

Price points to consider

I've seen one Internet marketer – Eben Pagan – offer a ten thousand dollar product online. I'm sure there has been others that I haven't seen, but this is what I've noticed. The number of closes go up on high priced items when there is a consultant to talk with about the purchase.

This is how I see it:

Anything up to $2,000 can be sold purely through online marketing.

Anything above that price point, unless you are an unbelievably exceptional copywriter and marketer, needs a conversation.

Our programs start at $5,000. We definitely make sure we talk to everyone who inquires with us. We're not leaving it to a sales page to do the selling for us when a conversation with a real person can make the decision so much easier for the client.

Plus, we want our prospects to have an experience of us. We're fun. We're playful. We like to laugh. We give our prospects an experience that they remember and they want to come back. I haven't seen a sales page, unless it's by Frank Kern, achieve this.

And we're not Frank Kern.

Bonus material:

For a
template of questions
to ask to prepare for a launch go to:

THE COACHING
INSTITUTE

www.smallbusinessmastermindclub.com.au/business-success

16

Unlocking the hidden backend profits in your business

For many businesses, having a backend product determines whether your business succeeds or not. You must have a specific backend in mind whenever you are planning your web site, choosing a product, or designing a product.

TERRY DEAN

Before I stumbled upon this gold mine I was doing just fine. It didn't even occur to me to think of the lifetime value of the client. It certainly didn't occur to me to design an entire marketing system for my existing clients.

When I did figure it out, I realised I had left a few million dollars on the table.

What is the "back end"?

The back end is the money that you can make from upselling and cross selling to your existing clients.

That first purchase is a 'transaction'. Transaction sales are the front end sales, and should be only half of your revenues.

The other half, or more, should come from upselling and cross selling to clients.

We have clients who start in our Certificate IV in Life Coaching. They can upgrade to the Diploma of Life Coaching. There are other upgrades and cross sells, including products, a membership site, NLP training, and Mastermind.

If you deliver great value and that first product is an exact match to your avatar – and as a guide, you should aim to deliver 3 times more value than the price of the investment – then your avatar will love what you deliver.

If they love that first product it makes sense that they should know about your second and third products too. After all, if they are passionate about the thing you offer, they aren't going to stop with one purchase. They will want to make a number of purchases, and if you don't offer them something more, they will get something more from someone else.

That's crazy.

Think about it. Do you only buy one book on a subject you love? Is this your only book or product on marketing and business success? Will it be your last ever? Of course not.

It's the same for your market. They will want more, and as long as you provide value and a match for their wants, they'll get it from you.

How to make staggering profits from the back end

Every good marketer I know has their back end in place and working well. We did $18,000 in upgrades today, whilst I'm writing this book. And we'll do the same tomorrow.

We have a few ways to make this happen:

Strategy #1: Prelaunch through emails

This strategy uses the launch techniques we've already learned. It's the most hands-off strategy there is, but also has the lowest success rate. Having said that, if you prefer to not have a team then it's definitely the way to go.

Strategy #2: Prelaunch through emails and teleclasses

A mixture of emails to the launch and then a series of classes works really well. Because it's got the human interaction, the client has more opportunity to have an experience of you and you get to tailor make what you say based on feedback you get on the calls.

We run "Bootcamp" classes and run a series of emails to do this. We deliver phenomenal value – clients get up to 16 clients in less than four weeks, which more than pays for the upgrade.

Strategy #3: Outbound phone calls

This is the best strategy, especially when it's combined with the previous two techniques. Nothing replaces a personal chat, where the call can be completely shaped according to the client's special wants and desires. It's highly recommended to do this for larger priced items.

Strategy #4: Sell from the stage

I love this technique because of its success.

You run an event – free or paid – and at the event you offer another product or service to the clients there.

I know one business that did $2.3 million in one weekend doing this.

PART III:

How to build the systems to get you out of your business

17

How to build a business that works for you so you don't kill yourself working for it

A boat doesn't go forward if each one is rowing their own way.

SWAHILI PROVERB

One of the secrets to establishing and running a successful business is to systemise anything that happens routinely and to only spend your time doing the one-offs or exceptions.

I know, you're probably thinking that systems are something only the big corporations have because their businesses are complex, large and they have thousands of people. You're probably thinking that your business doesn't lend itself to systemisation because it is so, well, straight forward or simple. If this is what you're thinking right now, don't worry because you're not alone. The vast majority of business owners think just like you.

This also happens to be one of the major reasons most business owners work so hard in their business and don't get to enjoy the lifestyles they should. You see, they work because their businesses don't. It's as simple as that. And the key to turning this around – so the business owner doesn't have to work because the business does – is to introduce systems.

Every system is designed with the outcome in mind. Think of them as a 'process' that is determined by 'purpose'. It should answer the question: for what purpose are we doing this?

Sometimes someone will forget or not know why a system was created, and want to change it to suit what they think is going on at the time, but if we bring it back to 'for what purpose' the decision is clear. For example, someone wanted to be paid more money for an event they were assisting with – we pay a token amount to say thanks for coming back – but no pay is actually due as it's considered a privilege to be invited back into the room, to re-experience the training event and help the new participants. The token amount was calculated at an hourly rate, but the person complained all because the original intent of the pay was lost.

Systems reside in a businesses' operations manual. That it where you go to look up any system the business has. Our operations manual contains sections for each part of the business:

- Administration
- Finance
- Sales
- Marketing
- Student support
- RTO management
- Event management

Each department has an operations manual, with lots of 'how to' documents written in MS Word for easy updates, and in Camtasia when it is better to have someone walking you through the steps of a system on the screen to see it in action.

All systems are updated each month (where needed), which means they will undergo an ongoing review process. Where a system needs updating, it either gets included in the goals for that month or it gets done on the spot in real time, whichever is more appropriate. The whole business is run on 90-day goals, so everyone has 90-day goals to achieve things that are proactive and will move the business forward. This stops reactive decision-making.

In a business that is reasonably complex, there can be a tendency for people to get caught up in the day-to-day reactions and bushfire management – which can stop all progress unless goals are in place. So each month, 90-day goals are produced, which are then broken down into one-month goals, and then weekly tasks.

So everyone becomes involved in playing a part in moving the business forward by working on their department's systems.

Let me explain how a system is typically updated by giving you an actual example from my business.

In events, one event operations manual might be rewritten once a member of the team attends an event and sees what has to be improved. Then, a month later, we might review how we book venues.

All suggested system improvements in student support and events go into the CANI register – the Constant and Never Ending Improvements Register – which gets added to as a result of feedback from the trainers, crew heads, crew and participants. All feedback that improves how to deliver to our clients goes into this register and is actioned throughout the month as part of the systems upgrades.

If a major system is changed or a policy developed, it goes into the Policy Review Folder and circulated around the office for everyone to review and sign off that they have read and understood it.

Each system is recorded on the computer for all to access. Hard copies of systems used often are turned into checklists. So, for an event, there is a checklist that starts four months before and counts down with what has to happen and when. All the steps are placed in the team member's calendar and they pop up when they need to be actioned.

Given that in any four-month period we have 12 or more events, this amounts to a lot of pop-ups, so accuracy is the key.

When the pop-up is actioned, it gets crossed off the checklist that was printed out for that one event. This goes on for all the events every day.

There is also a hard copy detailed system for each event, including photos of how to set the room up, thorough instructions on what links need to be sent to participants before the event, and drafts of all emails that need to be sent to the participants.

We have a system for contacting all participants every 90 days to see how they're going and if there is anything we can do for them. This is to find out if there's anything missing, to provide connection with our participants, to let them know what cool stuff we have coming up that they can join in with, and a way to check how they're progressing with their assessments.

We also have a system for free classes, which participants can attend. This gives them the opportunity to accelerate their results through hand-holding, accountability, and brainstorming on how to get clients. Incidentally, they tell us this is a great success.

Our systems are run in three areas:

- Get clients – sales and marketing
- Keep clients – student support, events
- Get paid by clients – finance and relationship management

The whole thing is focused on achieving these three things all the time and is managed in real time. We have hundreds of participants with different needs and wants, so we need to be creative, innovative and flexible about what we're willing to provide.

The process is that if we have to do something more than once, a system needs to be designed.

The professional development of team members is a system too – we interview all team members and find out what they want to focus on as part of their development for the year, and build an action plan for this so they can develop themselves personally and professionally.

The whole place is a demanding environment to work in. When we interview people, they say they want a challenge – then, when they get into the role, they realise they didn't know what 'challenge' meant, and quit fast.

People who come from places where they were not accountable find the environment really tough. People who don't like taking responsibility, don't last. People who get overwhelmed with long task lists, don't last.

Our turnover is high every time we expand our business. Our challenge is hiring for the job we need at the time, and also trying to make sure they have what it takes for the expansion that's coming; this can't be achieved when the job is task-focused – we know we will need a manager there.

There are a lot of part-timers in sales and student support because the ideal team member is a participant who can talk with confidence about the programs, how they work and how to make them work. This means we have too many people who join us for what they can learn from us while they build their own businesses.

That's another reason for our high turnover. We're only just getting to the point now – critical mass – where we have the size to justify non-coach administrators because, up until recently, even the administrator in student support needed to be able to answer coaching and marketing questions.

We are now fortunate to have a stable solid admin team who are not coaches but dedicated to admin, so that's improved things tremendously.

I have known for years where we needed to be, but we were never the size to justify having people who couldn't help students when they phoned, but could only do the behind-the-scenes stuff.

We tend to hire part-time coaches because they prefer this so they can work on their own businesses. So we split the day into two shifts to accommodate this.

We are only now at the point where we are finding people from our programs who will work full time and are dedicated to the role rather than their coaching career; I always knew this would take time.

The biggest challenge we have is finding someone to manage student support; someone who has been through the advanced programs (so he or she can answer any question), is accredited (to assist with assessments), can organise and manage 50 events a year, and can manage a growing team.

This area is where we are least stable, and have constantly managed it by dividing the role into smaller roles. Fortunately, this has worked well in the past. We have one person who is incredibly capable at events and assessments, and we have someone who is great at all things to do with students.

I can see the time coming when we will grow again, and this won't cut it. The question then becomes: can the current team handle the expansion, which inevitably comes and causes challenges and new pressures?

We have been in a state of rapid growth, so we still don't know what the final team model will look like. With programs that are entrepreneurial, and encourage 'having a go' and putting yourself out there, it's a challenge to hire people with these same qualities who even want a job. People with these qualities want to work for themselves – and anyone who wants to work for us full time, tends to not have these qualities and, thus, finds it a challenge to help the students in the same manner as the trainers do.

Our challenge is to find a balance between constantly training and communicating to the support team the importance of the style of communication. Using DISC, for example, student support team members tend to be more 'S' and 'C', whereas the trainers and the sales consultants are 'I' and 'D'.

So, it's important to manage the transition from being enrolled to being supported – and not have the new participant experience a major shift in gears and feel disappointed. To manage this we have 'Your Personal Success Planning Session'. This is a half-hour interview with a member of the student support team who will find out the participant's goals, dreams, values and expectations. By doing this, it helps the participant move their relationship from the sales consultant to the student support team, to feel assured that the support extends way beyond the 'sale', and to start to forge relationships with the team that they will work in.

We also have a quirky character in the student support team whose role it is to help our participants get clients, and then help them upgrade to the more advanced programs. This person needs to be 'quirky' because they become a personality – the character – that people are easily drawn to. The adventurous spirit we encourage in our participants needs to be in this person, so the participants can feel confident the character can help them grow their businesses.

The more interesting this person is, the better he or she can help. It's all strategic, difficult to achieve, a constant work in progress, and never perfect. I never compromise what it is we want to achieve. I'd never settle for a beige person in the quirky accountability role, and I'd never put an adventurous participant behind the scenes doing emails.

It's about balancing the priorities and keeping my eye on what we want to achieve, always without compromise. And it is in the system that I make this clear, so anyone running a job interview session knows this and bears it in mind.

Sometimes this means months of not having the right person in a role, which is frustrating for the participants – but the wrong person in a role would do more harm than good and cause more problems.

Our vision and culture statement is up on the walls for everyone to see – but the unwritten ground rules are that it's all about the students; they come first, and we don't make decisions that make things easier for us – we make decisions that make it better for them.

Because we're a personal development school, it can become interesting when it's time to collect payments and someone has defaulted. To make things easy for the finance department, and to ensure that this doesn't become personal, we have systemised how outstanding payments are collected. It becomes part of the process. Sometimes we get told that we should be 'caring' and not expect to demand a payment that's due – our policy is uncompromising on this: where a service is delivered, we expect to be paid. It has nothing to do with our being 'caring'; we're a business that has delivered, the same as any other business, and we expect our contracts to be honoured. Systems have helped us keep it on this level.

The company has reached that interesting milestone where it's no longer 'small', but it's not 'big' business either – it needs a strong and organised manager, and I've stepped aside to make sure this happens.

My strength is in the setting up and building of the business. Once it's got systems in place and most problems have been solved, I find my interest has waned and I'm better off getting out of the way and letting professional managers do their thing. My involvement now is to mentor team members, including the General Manager, and to solve problems that are new and until the team knows how. I see my role as helping people learn how to make great decisions, rather than making all the decisions myself.

I know I don't want to be there each day, and haven't been for years. From the beginning it was my goal to build a business that I didn't need to be involved in – and my involvement now is to run just a couple of the more advanced trainings, which is how I like it.

I am still too involved in the marketing because this is the hardest role in the whole business; and our marketing, because it's based on value-based marketing, needs a strong character the market can relate to and who knows the programs backwards.

In all our years of doing this, it was me until recently. I don't know if this is a good thing or a limiting factor, but it worked. Marketing is the last thing I would delegate – it's just too important.

Every business has its own peculiarities and ways of doing things. But this doesn't mean they can't use systems. You can even have a system for opening up the office in the morning and closing up in the evening. Think of it this way: even for such a simple task, how would a temp know what to do if the person who usually does this is off sick for six weeks? Where are the keys kept? Is there an alarm that needs to be deactivated in the morning and activated at night? What is the code? Do all the office lights get put on in the morning and switched off at night? If so, by whom? First person in, and last one out? Or just one person? Are there spare keys? If so, where are they kept?

So, assuming you have a routine task like this that you want to system-ise, how do you go about it?

Start by writing a description of the workflow. This needn't be elaborate: dot points will do. Just follow the process from beginning to end. Itemise each function or thing that is done, and make sure to include the reason (the outcome). Then include everything that can go wrong, and what should be done if that happens.

Remember, when you are systemising your business, you need to make sure you have the right environment for this to be taken seriously. Don't pay lip service to it; it will backfire if you do.

You also need to ensure that you have good, open lines of communication in the business. This is, after all, a team effort. The point of doing this is so that you don't have to do everything yourself, remember? So take it seriously and be supportive, giving genuine feedback to your team all the time.

Involve everyone in your business. This is something that not only affects everyone: it is also something *for* everyone. You see, the best person to write a system for a particular function is the person who usually carries out that function. They know it intimately and will spot weaknesses, shortcuts or better ways of doing things.

Involving everyone without giving them true responsibility is also going to lead to problems. So delegate well and trust them with the job. You did, after all, hire them to do the job, didn't you? And you chose them because, at the time, they were the best there was. So give them some responsibility and easy yourself out of the way.

Bonus material:

For a checklist of
how to design a system
go to:

www.smallbusinessmastermindclub.com.au/business-success

18

How to get the right people at the right time doing the stuff that counts

Teamwork is the fuel that allows common people to attain uncommon results.

UNKNOWN

One of the milestones any business reaches as it shakes off its initial growing pains is hiring its first real employee – or team member, as I like to call them. You see, this can really be thought of as a milestone because up until this point, the owner of the business will have been doing everything for him or herself. The business owner would have been wearing all the hats in the business: owner, production director, marketing director, sales director, finance director, bookkeeper, janitor, office clerk, telephonist, receptionist – the list goes on.

Just because a business is in its infancy and is only a one-man show doesn't mean that it only has one position in it. All the traditional (or usual) functions that larger and more established businesses have still need to be done at the start-up, albeit on a smaller scale.

As the business gets more settled and begins sourcing clients and actually doing business, what happens is this: the business owner becomes very good at managing, and doing, all the functions – often at the same time.

You know what this leads to, don't you? Proficiency. That's right, business owners become really good at carrying out tasks on a regular basis.

And what's more, because it's their own business, they think of it as 'their baby' and become quite attached to it. It's only natural because they instinctively see the link between doing the work and reaping the rewards through the business.

Then, over time, all the time, effort, energy and dedication they have been putting into the business begins to pay off. The business starts to grow.

Sure, there are often growing pains that accompany this, but that's only natural. Passionate business owners usually tackle this with relish. The result is twofold: the business begins to take off on the one hand, and the business owner becomes swamped on the other. There just doesn't seem to be enough time in the day to get everything done. So something suffers. It might be the business owners' health. It might be the level of service they pride themselves on. Or it might be that they become sloppy in most areas of the business, which results in clients becoming dissatisfied and going elsewhere.

The net result is that the business suffers.

The business owner then finds himself or herself between a rock and a hard place. Very often there just isn't enough money to take on an employee. Furthermore, the business owner usually can't find what it takes to actually let go and entrust someone else to take charge of certain aspect of the business and do things.

I guess it's much like letting go of your grown-up children as they move out of the family home.

All sorts of questions race through the business owner's mind. Things like 'can I afford this?' and 'he simply can't do the job to my standards and the clients will complain' are common.

The time comes with any growing business that employing the first team member simply can't be put off any longer. Once the business owner comes to this realisation, a new lot of uncertainties enter into the equation. Things like how to find the right person, how to know when the right one has been found, how to decide what to pay them, how to keep them excited and motivated once they are on board, and how to get the most out of them without exploiting them. A second layer of uncertainties then kicks in, with issues like 'can they be trusted to do the right things as far as the business and its goals are concerned'.

As anyone who has built up a business before will know, these are serious concerns that keep one awake at night. But they are also concerns that simply have to be tackled head on. The good news is, of course, that once you have worked through it, you will invariably wonder why you worried so much about it before.

For those who are still wrestling with these issues, listen to what the many who have gone through them before have to say. There is, after all, no need for you to reinvent the wheel to find you own way through this minefield if others have mapped the way for you to follow. That really does make sense, from a business point-of-view.

Get a business coach and let them assist you. They have the experience of countless examples and have helped many others do it efficiently and well.

Learning from others has always been a great philosophy to have, I believe. So, with this in mind, let me give you a run down on how we go about hiring team members in my business.

To start with, we don't use recruiters; it's never worked for us in the past. In keeping with our approach to technology, we use SEEK (www. seek.com.au) and word of mouth. We find word of mouth to be particularly powerful because, in general, people like recommendations based on personal experience. They know that traditional advertising is 'biased' and that very often the job isn't anything like the ad said it was. Also, recruiters so often don't care about the applicant as much as they do about their client, and it shows. Job applicants are so often given the run around and left dangling without knowing if their application has made it to the next round or not. I just don't like this way of going about things.

Once we receive a response from our ad, the next thing we need to think about it how to select the best, or most suitable, person for the job. How much weight should we put on their CVs? We hire for attitude rather than experience, unless there is a specific skill we are after. We believe that anyone can learn the specifics of a job, but the attribute we value most is what's in their heart and sole. Are they enthusiastic with a good work ethic? Are they happy, lively and bubbly? Will they fit in with the rest of the team? These are the important things.

As so much of what we need is based in direct marketing and psychology, there is rarely a skill set match, so it's more about attitude. We look for people who have a genuine appreciation of what a 'challenge' means, so they will have faced ongoing challenges and done well, they will enjoy variety, find it effortless talking with a wide range of people, and they'll love innovation.

When it comes to the general character type we usually look for, we want a person who would get bored if they had five minutes spare in the day. They would think it's beneath them to have a structured, repetitive day. They would always think of others, rather than fear for themselves.

It's important that everyone in our business 'clicks' with each other. They must agree with our culture. This means they would enjoy a good laugh and be a little crazy. In fact, they would instigate craziness from time to time.

Our people love that we sing *Happy Birthday* as well as a song that suits the person when it's their birthday, with no backup music. When something needs doing, they're onto it; they don't hang back.

Another common characteristic of our 'dream' team member is that they complain that their previous boss was not demanding enough of them. They don't complain about their old bosses as being poor bosses, just that they were not helping them be busy enough.

They speak highly of whatever area of specialty they're going into. For instance, admin people want to be great at admin, and don't want to move onto something more interesting when it comes along.

Some other things we look for are that:

1. they can easily give examples of where they have shown initiative; it's not a struggle

2. they speak loyally of their previous employment

3. they are articulate, friendly and not shy

4. they would welcome having the chance to get feedback, and when asked what they are afraid of, they answer 'being bored'

Poor candidates say they don't like being criticised when asked how they respond to feedback; they are old-school and not used to getting feedback. This is a real problem for us, as everyone can always improve. The world is moving ahead whether we like it or not, so unless we move forward too, we will find ourselves stagnating or, worse still, going backwards. And this is not someone we want in our company because our very nature is to be at the forefront and leading the pack.

What we look for more than anything else is a cultural fit – the right attitude is friendly, helpful, down to earth, very articulate (both written and verbal), and able to demonstrate innovation.

That is what we look for to start with. Think of it as the first filter. Those who don't meet these basic or fundamental characteristics are filtered off. Then we get more specific with those who remain.

If we are recruiting someone for sales, we want someone who is outgoing, an 'I' on DISC, overly driven by money and ambitious. Our ideal consultant is able to talk to anyone about anything anytime.

This type of person is harder to find that you would think. They can have 'D' in them but not on the outside. They need to be able to learn quickly, focus on the other person and not their own concerns, and stay disciplined enough to do what it takes to succeed. While we do have a full sales system, it still takes flair, personality and character to close the sales.

When it comes to hiring someone to work in student support, we're more looking for someone who is an 'S' with DISC – someone who has long relationships, draws people around them, has an eye for detail, is able to follow instructions, who is always able to go the extra mile, and welcomes ways to give more and help more.

Our ideal admin type is a 'C' with 'S': they have huge attention to detail, can multitask, and are about to talk and shoot at the same time while singing the Aussie anthem. They understand that the client comes first, but that they need to be an interesting leader for the client to follow. They need to be able to inspire the client to succeed.

Nearly all of what we do, which influences who we hire, is around the psychology of value-based marketing. We are marketing to prospects. We are marketing to students. And our administration markets through their efficiency.

It's all marketing, just with different perspectives, so it's important the team is professional, outgoing, helpful and inspiring. We are large enough now that we hire dedicated admin people, so some of the leadership may get lost as we move forward; but, generally, most our team have leadership attributes.

Using my example, think about how it applies to your business. Are there any similarities? How can you use this example to generate ideas that will fit your own particular situation?

Can you see how taking a considered, highly targeted focus will only make the job of finding the 'someone' with the right credentials easier? Can you see the importance of selecting based on attitude? Can you see how important it is for that new person to fit in with the existing culture of your business?

Once you have a good idea about the particular attributes someone needs to have for the various roles within your business, it then becomes a fairly simple matter to take this to the next level by systemising your recruiting process.

Afterword

A real decision is measured by the fact that you've taken a new action. If there's no action, you haven't truly decided.

TONY ROBBINS

The possibilities are endless

Back in 2003, I thought I was a business owner, but I wasn't – I had a job. It was me doing everything, with no end in sight.

My success was my failure – I had so many one-on-one clients who wanted time with me that I didn't have time for anything but coaching.

I had over 50 clients, and 20 of them were on a waiting list. Probably sounds like a dream come true, until you think about the cost of this on your life and your relationships.

I would get home on Friday completely exhausted, knowing I had to do it all over again the following week, and the week after that...

When I made the decision to find another way, I had no idea how much would change in my life. Or my finances.

I went from a million dollar year to doing a million dollar month – with less hours from me than I was doing when I was coaching.

That's crazy! It's fantastic!

But it took me committing to doing things in a way I had never considered before. I had to let go of the 'employee' mindset of trading time for money and figure out how to make the dollar without being in the room.

That's the puzzle I've solved.

And people starting asking me how I did it. A lot of people starting asking me. If I wasn't careful, I was going to be back selling my time for money all over again.

That's why I put the Mastermind Program together and that's why I wrote this book.

You don't have to do it how I did – paid by the hour, hour after hour.

How about instead, you stay home this Monday and write your book whilst over $40,000 in sales are done by other people?

How about you have life on your terms – you come and go as you please, you work where and when you want and you do what you want.

You have a life.

For most people, it's an urban legend – but if you've read this book, you know it's a possibility for you and your family.

If you're new to business, this book will guide you through the pitfalls and mistakes you want to avoid. It will help you discover what the exact steps are to building a successful business, on your terms.

If you're in business, it will make you realise that this is just the beginning and that you are about to boost your results, with the same or less effort.

If you're an employee looking for a way out, this book has in it everything you need to know so you can get free of the rat race in a way that is affordable and fun.

All the steps are there.

I wish you the best of luck with your business success.

I trust you enjoy living life on your terms.

And when it happens for you, email me at:

mastermindclub@thecoachinginstitute.com.au

I'd love to share your success story to the next 'hobbyist' who wants to build a business and have life on their terms.

Resources

Develop your millionaire mindset

The Success Principles, Jack Canfield
The Answer, John Assaraf and Murray Smith
Awaken the Giant Within, Tony Robbins
An Intelligent Life, Julian Short
The Outsider's Edge – The Making of Self-made Billionaires, Brent D Taylor
How to Make a Hell of a Profit and Still Get to Heaven, Dr. John F. Demartini

Develop your marketing expertise

Influence: The Psychology of Persuasion, Robert Cialdini
Yes: 50 Scientifically Proven Ways to Be Persuasive, Robert Cialdini
Subliminal Persuasion, Dave Lakhani
Predictably Irrational, Dan Ariely
Buy-ology, Martin Linstrom
Neuromarketing, Patrick Renvoise and Christophe Morin
Buying Trances, Joe Vitale
All Marketers Are Liars, Seth Godin
Web Copy That Sells, Maria Veloso
The Robert Collier Letter Book, Robert Collier
How To Make Money While You Sleep, Brett McFall
The E Code, Joe Vitale and Jo Han Mok
The Never Cold Call Again Online Playbook, Frank J. Rumbauskas Jr.

Our Internet Secrets, Andrew and Daryl Grant
Email Marketing, Malcolm Auld
www.smallbusinessmastermindclub.com.au, Sharon Pearson
www.andrewanddarylgrant.com, Daryl and Andrew Grant
www.masscontrol.com, The Legendary Frank Kern
www.productlaunchformula.com, Jeff Walker
www.ourinternetsecrets.com, Andrew and Daryl Grant

Develop your business skills

Good to Great, Jim Collins
The Breakthrough Company, Keith R. McFarland
The One Minute Manager Builds High Performing Teams, Ken Blanchard
The E-Myth Revisited, Michael Gerber
www.thecoachinginstitute.com.au, Sharon Pearson
www.youcanreadanyone.com.au, Joe Pane

Web resources from the book

www.smallbusinessmastermindclub.com.au
www.smallbusinessmastermindclub.com.au/case-studies
www.smallbusinessmastermindclub.com.au/business-success
www.scrapbookingprofits.com
www.yoga-teacher-training.com
www.wordtracker.com
www.googlekeywordtool.com
www.clickbank.com
http://groups.google.com
www.ourinternetsecrets.com
www.thecoachinginstitute.com
www.y2agency.com/monopolize.html
www.tubemogul.com
www.dotcomsecrets.com
www.andrewanddaryl.com
www.seek.com.au

Testimonials for Sharon Pearson and the Mastermind Program

If business is your second name then mastermind is the course for you. After working hard for years, mastermind taught us to work smarter, not harder! As a business owner of 2 companies, I mainly joined mastermind for my Style/Coaching company "Trend Style and Coaching", which I now hold Image Workshops, with more workshops to come. This has doubled my profits.

We also run a Horizontal Drilling Company. I didn't realise what I would learn in mastermind I could apply to this company, which installing the skills learnt from the course we made huge changes. These changes have enabled our company to increase the gross profit by over $1,000,000 for the past 6 months.

Don't hesitate to work smarter, not harder! Thank you to Sharon and everyone from TCI. Life is "fabulous".

CAROLYN ROWLAND, TREND STYLE AND COACHING

I am literally generating leads in my sleep!!

Before Mastermind I had a good business with limited success, I generated approx 7-9 leads in 6 months; after Mastermind I generated 69 leads in 6 days!!! Not only have my leads increased, but I also earned my entire course fees back in less than a week after completing the 5 day event and I'm really excited to share that I have just had my first $50,000 month - oh and we are only half way through the month... what more can I achieve? - whatever I choose to!

Thanks to Sharon and the team I am now running the business I have always dreamed of. I have booked my first holiday since starting my business and I am really thrilled about what the future holds. I generate leads in my sleep, what more can small business owners ask for??

NAOMI ALDRED, NEXUS COACHING GROUP

The Small Business Mastermind Program significantly added to our body of knowledge in business and marketing, and has enabled us to pursue avenues and opportunities that previously we weren't aware existed. We've been able to easily combine this knowledge into our existing framework and earn the same annual income with only expending half the amount of time. This enables us to live life on our terms, and run our businesses how we choose for the results we desire. If you are a small business owner looking to increase your income, expand your opportunities and reclaim your time, we highly recommend you take a look at the Small Business Mastermind Program and see how it can benefit you.

OWEN & CLARE COPE, CAPABILITY DEVELOPMENT SOLUTIONS

When I first looked into Mastermind, I had a very successful business which was keeping me a bit too busy. I needed a solution that would allow me to generate a passive income stream that didn't mean I needed to be present for the dollars to come in. I was looking for a way of achieving the dream life style that my business was meant to create when I left corporate. After completing Mastermind, I had a totally new perspective on the shape and strategies for my business and had identified a new niche that needed my skills and which could be delivered through innovative formats and didn't require me in the room. I am in the processes of launching Small Business Wizard; I have had incredible feedback so far and am really looking forward to seeing where this new venture will take me!

JULI ROBERTSON, JTB CONSULTING PTY LTD

I get up every single morning, with a constant energised buzz in my heart, mind and body. I am inspired, excited and uncompromisingly certain about my future, unlike ever before. I don't look back, I don't even look sideways. My vision is straight ahead, and the possibilities are AWESOME!

AMBER MCLEAN, MILLIONAIRE LAUNCH STUDIO

I have run my own businesses for 20 years, from Opera Singer to one of Australia's top Relationship Coaches and NLP Trainer. It has been a career of which I earned great money and felt I made a real difference to hundreds and hundreds of individuals and businesses.

That was before I did Mastermind. Before I even attended the closed door training, I sold my first product for over $30,000 in 10 minutes, just from what I learned in the pre-study material. I was speechless and awe-struck. At last I had found the key to "really" make a positive difference on a grand scale. I couldn't believe how easy it was and how congruent I felt to offer a product of such immense value that, since then has earned for others more than $100,000+ in their coaching fees and most importantly, as a result of this product, their clients are getting great results.

I have created another 2 products since then and I feel I have my life back again. I work the hours I choose and I have my office anywhere from the beach, to a cafe or at my beautiful ranch. As a mother to teenagers, I feel for the first time I can be really present for their needs right now. I am also on track to earn my first million without having to trade time for money. The journey has just begun and I love every minute of it! Thank you Sharon!

ALICE HAEMMERLE, A PERFECT MIND;
INSTANT INSIGHT COMMUNICATION SYSTEMS; ASKALICE.COM.AU

Mastermind changed my mind. At a time when all of my friends and colleagues are thinking about retirement I have launched into a new venture and established my own business. Mastermind effectively equipped me with the mindset, belief, tools and tribe I needed to take the steps necessary. I couldn't be happier with the results and thanks to Mastermind know I have only just started!!!

KEVIN LARKINS, LEADING AUSTRALIA

I own a small software business and had spent the last 6 years plugging away spending over 100 days a year on the road and 70 hours a week making sales. I knew there had to be an easier way and a way that I could systemise my whole process. Then I discovered Sharon Pearson's Mastermind program.

In just 3 months I have had a 500% increase in my lead generation and I have been able to cut my hours to between 6-8 per week with almost no travel and have created a system that is repeatable, measurable and effective. My sales are up 11% on the same time last year and I have been able to find tons of time to follow other passions. The Mastermind program has completely changed my life and Sharon has inspired me to even higher highs.

GLEN MURDOCH, MURDOCH COACHING

It was around that time that I heard about Mastermind and I was struck by this world of entrepreneurialism where creative minds and sophisticated strategies congregated that was not only inspiring but challenging. Plus, I got the best of International and Australian strategies all in one place which meant I didn't have to waste time separating the 'wheat from the chaff'. Before I made the decision to step, become a member of Mastermind we were earning the same income as the average Australian. But because of the strategies and support I have now because I am a Mastermind Member my new business billed $27,750 before even doing my 7 Day Closed Door which made back my Mastermind Investment nearly twice over. Within the next 68 days we started amping things up to get rid of our franchise business, which sold within 3 weeks because of a Mastermind strategy that we applied, plus during that time I happened to bill another $9,050. I now enjoy a business that because of the support, the systems, and the business partners I have in the Mastermind Club, in 8 weeks, we are taking our first, and long awaited holiday in 5 years but more importantly, I now only work 15 hours a week. I have my time back to be innovative in business, I am a stress free mum for my kids and I get to hang out and adore my husband again.

ILSE STRAUSS, OPTIMUM INFLUENCE

I have always believed I could achieve anything. I can't remember what motivated me to be in the room, but I am damn pleased I was. No book, no other program delivers the content, quality, challenges and success that this program has delivered. I look forward to sharing my results with everyone and building my LIST!!!

KRISTEN RISBY, BETTER RESULTS

I am thrilled with how things are going and I recognise that I have the confidence and skills due to the program. Meanwhile, my $10,000 deal has grown to a $23,000 deal, I have another $10,000 deal in the works - just waiting on a date to begin. I have work booked to October (and we're only in July!), have earned $30,000 in 3 months, with projected billings of $60,000 (not including the 'big deal') to end September, even if I take on no further projects.

LINDA MILLER

Before the 7-day closed door training, I had no clear idea as to the direction of my business and no idea of how to get my next client. By day one my niche was sorted and by day seven I had over 120 leads!

MIA MONTAGLIANI, YOUR DOG NEEDS YOU

I'm moving my family to New York City this month... BUT we're not "moving" the business we're EXPANDING it...

I made a six figure income in my FIRST year as a coach (thanks Sharon!). In the second year we've gone global -setting up The Leadership Coach LLC in the USA. And best of all funded our own not-for-profit in NYC that we're launching next month!

PAUL ANDREW, THE LEADERSHIP COACH

As a direct result of mastermind I have changed many paradigms around what it takes to have a successful business while having the time to enjoy life. I stopped working for the short term income and started planting the right seeds to create and maintain sustainable and profitable businesses for the long run.

I'm developing an e-learning project and online stores. Mastermind has given me the tools to do it and start making money without being present in my business.

KAREN VEGA, ENGINEERING OF RESULTS

My lifestyle has changed dramatically since being in the Mastermind group with Sharon Pearson. My mindset has completely changed and I now step by step on how to create the massive results in my business that I've always been striving for. I am now undertaking workshops, webinar programs, writing eBooks, among other things, and I believe none of this would be possible without the information I have received from Sharon and the rest of the Mastermind program.

My business is now set to double its annual turnover, and I couldn't be more pleased! The investment into Mastermind was as much in me, as it was in the information I was going to receive! I highly recommend this program to anybody who wants to achieve phenomenal results in their business! Sharon Pearson is the absolute Best person to learn and model from!

REBECCA HAWKINS, INSPIRED TO THRIVE

I commenced Mastermind at the end of April 2010 and completed my closed door training in early May 2010. 15 days later I successfully launched my 1st major product which sold 1200 copies and made over $250,000 in 4 days. I have not looked back since.

I have successfully negotiated and am currently in the midst of fine tuning a multi-million dollar deal to deliver coaching services Australia wide in my niche. Mastermind has given me both the tools and skills to succeed and the confidence to believe in myself and tweak my mindset to get excellent results every time. I am now working less hours face-to-face, have greater financial freedom and feel as though I am living the lifestyle I had always dreamed of.

DR NATALIE GREEN, BETTALIFE SOLUTIONS

From the very beginning there really was only one school. The Coaching Institute were genuinely interested in who I was, my goals and had the same high standards I wanted associated with my business now and into the future. The skills I am learning are making an immediate impact to help my clients, and are giving me the tools to grow what I believed was the best job in the world into something even bigger and better.

Truth be told, I haven't even begun to apply a fraction of what I'm learning and I've already had fabulous results. I've increased the joy and creativity I have in my work, assisted clients in some earth shattering transformations and in the last month ramped up my income by over $4000. This is just the beginning.

I thought that I was studying life coaching to help my clients achieve their dreams and as a complete bonus I have learned how to build my own.

LAURA BIRD, ONE SPIRIT

After searching extensively for months for a small business mentor I discovered Sharon Pearson's 'Mastermind'. I wanted a Sales and Marketing program that would give me the answers I needed to accelerate my business – fast. I had spent thousands of dollars making mistakes – I was determined to find an easier way. Within the first two months of training I had my niche nailed and I managed to secure my first $12,000 coaching contract with a Melbourne legal firm.

I now have the tools in my toolkit to earn passive income and live the life I choose.

AMANDA MALLIA, AMANDA MALLIA & ASSOCIATES

Since doing Mastermind I have learnt to market my business in a way that is current and up to date. Mastermind is so exciting it was a privilege to be in the room with an amazing and successful woman such as Sharon Pearson.

DALE BOURKE, 21ST CENTURY NLP